# KARMA WITHOUT STRESS

BOOKS BY EILEEN CONNOLLY

TAROT: A NEW HANDBOOK FOR THE APPRENTICE
    (THE CONNOLLY TAROT, VOL. I)
TAROT: THE HANDBOOK FOR THE JOURNEYMAN
    (THE CONNOLLY TAROT, VOL. II)
THE CONNOLLY BOOK OF NUMBERS, VOL. I: THE
    FUNDAMENTALS
THE CONNOLLY BOOK OF NUMBERS, VOL. II: THE
    CONSULTANT'S MANUAL
EARTHDANCE (A novel)
KARMA WITHOUT STRESS: CONNOLLY ESOTERIC
    GUIDEBOOKS, VOL. I

Forthcoming:

TAROT: THE HANDBOOK FOR THE MASTER
    (THE CONNOLLY TAROT, VOL. III)
KARMA, NUMBERS AND THE DESTINY OF CHILDREN
CONNOLLY ESOTERIC GUIDEBOOKS:
    VOL. II: PSYCHIC DEVELOPMENT
    VOL. III: FORMS OF HEALING
    VOL. IV: THE BODIES OF MAN
    VOL. V: THE MYSTICAL GATE
    VOL. VI: APPROACHING THE CABALA

# CONNOLLY ESOTERIC GUIDEBOOKS
## VOLUME I

# KARMA WITHOUT STRESS
# A GUIDEBOOK FOR THE SOUL'S JOURNEY

EILEEN CONNOLLY

NEWCASTLE PUBLISHING CO., INC.
North Hollywood, California
1989

Edited by Douglas Menville
Connolly Tarot illustrations by Peter Paul Connolly
Cover Design by Riley K. Smith

Illustrations of seven of the Major Arcana from the Connolly Tarot Deck are reproduced herein through the permission of U.S. Games Systems, Inc.

This book is not intended to diagnose, prescribe, or treat any ailment, nor is it intended in any way as a replacement for medical consultation when needed. The author and publishers of this book do not guarantee the efficacy of any of the methods herein described, and strongly suggest that at the first suspicion of any disease or disorder the reader consult a physician.

FIRST EDITION
A NEWCASTLE BOOK
First printing, October 1989
10  9  8  7  6  5  4  3  2
Printed in the United States of America

WITH LOVE
to Mary Alice and James Thomas Holmes

I dedicate this book to my parents. In the beginning I saw and felt the challenge of life. As a child I seldom understood my own motivations or theirs. As I grew I often felt separated and isolated. I had periods of apprehension regarding things I had done and had not done. I look back with hindsight and regretfully see that I was sometimes right!

Only maturity brings the vision to see how the needle of experience strongly pierces the delicate karmic pattern each of us weaves. I recognize and appreciate the love that was given. I know my parents felt what all parents feel for their children. Each of us, in our own way, convey what we can to our young. I smile sadly and sometimes feel sorry for the little girl who tried to weave against the weft.

# CONTENTS

# LIST OF MAJOR ARCANA

# LIST OF ESOTERIC EXERCISES

# LIST OF KARMIC MEDITATIONS

# THE CONNOLLY ESOTERIC GUIDEBOOKS

This is the first volume in a new series of books for the esoteric scholar. Six volumes are planned for *The Connolly Esoteric Guidebooks*, each having its own focus on a different area of parapsychology. They are intended to provide a format for basic study and broad comprehension in each area.

As with all my books, my intention is to teach you as simply as possible how to work with and understand basic esoteric concepts. Whatever your purpose in studying may be, these books will provide you with a continual ready reference. Both teachers and students will find the series helpful and informative.

My previous books have served this same purpose through the years, as I have been told by many scholars and teachers I have had the pleasure to meet throughout the world. I continue to think of you all as I write these pages, and my love and encouragement goes out to you in your progress on the Path of Life.

Future volumes in this series will be entitled:

*Psychic Development* (Vol. II)
*Forms of Healing* (Vol. III)
*The Bodies of Man* (Vol. IV)
*The Mystical Gate* (Vol. V)
*Approaching the Cabala* (Vol. VI)

I hope you will find this series of Esoteric Guidebooks helpful in your journey toward the Light.

# PREFACE

*Karma Without Stress* contains esoteric philosophy, methods and procedures for recognizing and alleviating the karmic origins of stress in our lives. It is intended for students, consultants and teachers.

By learning and using the simple methods of meditation and esoteric exercise presented here you will quickly learn how to discover the sources of stress in your life and understand how they relate to your karmic destiny. You will find that the philosophy and meditations in this book will be of great assistance in overcoming personal barriers. They can be utilized equally well by an individual or in group studies.

In this book, I hope to teach you as simply as possible how to proceed toward ridding your life of Karmic Stress. I would like you to feel that I am teaching you personally, so that this esoteric study becomes not only a source of learning but a friend you can relate to on a very personal level.

From your continual and very welcome correspondence, I know that my books have become old friends to many of you. Yesterday's students have now become teachers, having found the seed of knowledge in my first book, and having carefully nurtured it into a brilliant bloom whose fragrance fills the soul.

To all my readers and friends throughout the world, I give my most sincere thanks. You do me much honor. I hope that the present volume will prove a welcome addition to your libraries.

Eileen Connolly
Virginia
December 1988

# INTRODUCTION

This book presents an entirely new approach to the much-discussed problem of stress in modern life. It marries this concept to the age-old concept of karma in order to produce a totally new way of looking at the problems in our lives. Today the average adult is subjected to a tremendous amount of stress in many different areas of life. We become concerned about every ache and pain, fearful that it may signal something worse. We are constantly bombarded with information and advice about what kinds of food to eat, whether or not they are safe to eat, how much exercise we should engage in and a thousand other worries. Our bodies may be healthier, but the stress factor remains, causing an underlying unhappiness and discontent.

Karma is seldom associated with a sense of well-being. Our attention turns to the concept only when we feel it may be involved in our problems in this life. This book is intended to allow you to explore a number of karmic possibilities. It aims to open a wide vista of self-therapy and healing, so that you can eliminate the karmic origins of the stress in your life.

It is my contention that all negativity is associated with imbalanced karma. This situation, which occurs to some degree in almost everyone at one time or another, can cause tremendous stress within a person. Among the many definitions of stress in the dictionary are "emphasis," "importance" and "intense strain." All of these definitions are applicable to our study. Karma is the Law of Cause and Effect. Here you will have the opportunity to go to the *original* cause to eliminate undesirable effects in your life. For most people, the cause of the troublesome effects in their lives is unknown.

We have progressed tremendously in the areas of medicine and science, yet we usually seek to correct the effect rather than find the true cause. This is at least partially because it is not always easy to locate the actual cause. But by utilizing the correct esoteric procedures, it is possible to reach the source of any present-day dilemma. Developing the desire to confront the source will eventually eliminate the negative effects of karma. The results can be quite surprising, for often the source, the reason for stress, unhappiness and unsatisfactory relationships, has no real connection to your current problems.

Only by developing self-discovery can you leave the source behind. All it requires is your personal determination to rid yourself of anxiety and to recognize the mystical threads of karma woven into your life.

Through the use of the simple esoteric procedures given in this book you will begin to see your original karmic intention unfold. Then life begins. As the ancient saying advises: *Gnothe seauton*—"Know thyself."

# CHAPTER 1

# UNDERSTANDING KARMA

Karma is life! Thoughts, words and actions all contribute to the karmic pattern. Known and unknown, seen and unseen, you weave your karmic thread. Although you may believe that others are responsible for your particular situations in life, destiny is very personal. The truth is, you are totally responsible.

The karmic thread must be flexible, allowing the life pattern to change in color, texture and design. Certain patterns may seem familiar—difficult and concentrated areas of your life may be a repetition of your previous efforts or lack of them.

Delving into karma may seem at first to be quite complex. But to simplify your karmic obligations, all you have to do is realize that they were predetermined by *you*. This realization will bring you to the beginning of understanding why each life path is so personal. Just imagine what your life would be like if it were *not* predetermined by you!

Once you are born you are locked into a life pattern that you consider beneficial to the journey of your soul. Before this life, you were the designer, programmer and engineer of this life pattern, working with a Higher Consciousness that could see beyond the limited vision of the physical plane. You planned your destiny before birth; then, at the moment of birth you relinquished this higher knowledge and submitted to the limited mechanism of the human brain. You then became confined to the lower levels of human consciousness and will remain there until you learn how to reconnect with your Higher Self.

## *DÉJÀ VU*

Extraordinary opportunities to explore ourselves via the Higher Consciousness are sometimes offered us through the phenomenon of *déjà vu*. When you experience the feeling that you have been at a certain place before or have known a certain person before, even though your rational mind tells you this is not true, you are experiencing *déjà vu*. Consider such incidents as red alert buttons, if you will. A situation, a person, a place, a smell can automatically press these buttons. When this occurs, you are being reminded of past-life patterns that are identical or relevant to your situation today. The same thing can happen in dreams.

Unfortunately, many people ignore these incidents, explaining them away as waking dreams or coincidence. This is too bad, for here is a way to tune in to your karmic motivation. Once you put aside your everyday emotions and thinking patterns, you will have the esoteric space to explore your karmic whys and wherefores.

What does all this mean? It simply means that if you will let go of your present emotional level and explore these incidents, you can access your higher levels of consciousness. You can learn to rise above your mundane circumstances and discover your karmic purpose.

## KARMIC REALITY

Each relationship, the place where you were born, who your parents were—all these have meaning beyond the casual and the mundane. Your inherent talents, your present occupation, the entire status of your life are the result of your own karmic determination—your karmic reality. Many people take a complicated approach to the concept of karma, when in reality it is very simple. Karma is your chosen life path—your need to grow spiritually and correct past inadequacies and imbalances. This is the goal of all people, whether they are conscious of it or not. Only through this need to advance and improve can we begin to understand the mystery of life and our purpose in God's plan.

You may feel that there are no answers; through the reality of karma there are many. If you feel that you are continually giving of yourself without receiving anything back, either to one person or many, perhaps this was your intent. Knowing when to sever a relationship is also a karmic decision. The usual remedy is to meet with a friend, discuss your problem and ask for advice. This is good therapy, but it is more important to take time to discuss your problem with yourself!

Only you can see the whole picture. You can rely on your Higher Self to be totally honest, even if *you* cannot. If you earnestly pursue and examine your own feelings, you will be forced to be honest with yourself—the truth of your situation will eventually come into focus. Only from this point can you make correct decisions. This can be a painful process—it can hurt your ego and alienate you from what you hold dear. But this means that you are making progress. Now you are facing karmic reality and being forced to make a definite choice for your best interests.

Not many people enjoy this self-cleansing process; too often they try to depend solely on others to tell them what to do. They attempt to avoid doing what they know they should do. This approach is useless, for it not only negates the possibility of correcting and healing past imperfections but adds to the weight of karmic responsibility.

If little children are afraid to look at something, they will often keep their eyes shut tight to avoid seeing it. Adults do the same thing when they are afraid to face karmic reality. In this book it is our quest to discover the many ways you can recognize karma in your life. You need to understand that the word "karma" need not have a negative connotation. Karma *is* life—your life, and by exploring the various levels of consciousness you can elevate and improve your karmic route down the Road of Destiny.

Imagine a world free from fear; a world in which you are able to accept any circumstances you may encounter and have the inner strength to rid yourself of all that is not beneficial to your life path. Karmic Meditation can bring you to this world. Your only limitations come from your conscious mind. A genuine urge to know and to be free will carry you beyond limitations into an exciting area of esoteric independence.

## KARMIC RELATIONSHIPS

Before you are born, your soul is attracted to your parents-to-be, especially the mother. It undergoes various stages of instruction to prepare it for incarnation on the physical plane. The soul endeavors to incarnate with other souls who have shared life experiences in previous existences. The perfect beginning to a new life is when a soul is able to follow the correct plan it has determined to be beneficial for its growth.

Unfortunately, this not always possible. Many obstacles can prevent this ideal situation. Since time as we know it here on earth is not the same as before birth, a soul attempting to be born to a particular family may not succeed. Various earthly considerations may prevent the birth, such as miscarriage, illness, birth control, etc. The prospective parents simply may not be ready for a child at the time the soul is ready to be born.

Another example might be a soul who is trying to correlate its new life with that of a "soul mate" from a previous life. The two life plans may not coincide for the best interests of both souls. A word here about "soul mates": We hear this term used frequently, usually with a romantic connotation. We think of a pair of souls irresistably drawn to each other as lovers in life after life, destined never to part. Actually, a soul mate can reincarnate as a parent, grandparent, friend or sibling as often as a life partner. The human emotions adjust to the karmic relationships according to the earthly relationships. The perfect union between two souls can take the form of any kind of relationship on the physical plane.

The earthly consciousness which controls the emotional level here on earth establishes the kind of relationship that will exist, according to the nature of the relationship. This can cause distress as well as happiness, depending on how the two souls adapt to the relationship established in this life.

One of the most puzzling and disturbing aspects of karmic relationships concerns babies or young children who die at a very early age. It seems harsh and senseless, yet it is karmically normal. We try to rationalize the reason for such a terrible occurrence, but the real reason must be sought beyond the physical.

A soul can choose to enter the earth life for only a brief period entirely for the benefit of the parents' karma. A soul who did not live out its allotted life span in a previous life may come back to finish that time in a new life. This would indicate the completion of a karmic pattern for both the soul and its parents.

There is a moment in earthly time when a soul's life span ends. This particular moment is a part of the overall plan. When a soul does not fulfill the preplanned time period, it may return for a short time in conjunction with the karma of others. This often occurs with souls who had previous lives as soldiers, accident or murder victims, etc. This doesn't mean that immediately after death the soul elects to come back right away. The new incarnation could occur many years later, as we know time.

## INTERCHANGERS

A lesser-known variation of premature death and rebirth occurs in the case of what I call INTERCHANGERS. Sometimes souls who had a short life span in one life will voluntarily interchange with another soul in the present life. This agreement is made on the esoteric plane and is completely voluntary on the part of both souls. The reason for the second soul to take over when the first soul leaves the body is to enable the second soul to complete a situation it was unable to finish in the previous life. Usually an Interchanger stays near a dying body well before actual death occurs. It is possible that the departing soul is aware of these circumstances; perhaps the two souls converse mentally even though the body may be very ill. Often this situation is misunderstood by the family and friends of the dying person; they assume he is talking to someone "on the other side."

When the ill person miraculously recovers his health, the family and friends are unaware that his soul has departed. They do not realize that the soul they knew has "died." They discover that certain personality traits they were accustomed to are no longer there. Soon they become familiar with the new soul and its new ways, feeling that because the loved one was at death's door he is now expressing a hidden side of his personality which was not previously manifested.

Prior to the takeover by the Interchanger there is usually a long sleep or state of unconsciousness. Upon awaking from this condition the new soul—the Interchanger—adapts very quickly to the new body, although a good deal of effort is required to adjust to this body and the action of new brain cells.

I have been asked how such a situation could occur without the knowledge of those nearest and dearest to the person. The answer is that the incoming soul uses the same vocal cords to speak; he has spent a great deal of time in the aura field of the first soul and has become quite familiar with the life and history of that soul.

Some Interchangers retain their memories and are aware that they are taking over a new body. They may or may not remember the reason for it. Others do not retain the memory; for them it is like a new birth.

We can think of Interchanging as a normal method of acquiring rebirth. Something has existed between two souls prior to this event and they have mutually predecided that this takeover should occur. An Interchanger usually has a deep need to complete something, and the use of a mature physical body is ideal for this purpose.

## LOVE AND KARMA

Why is it that we think of the perfect love as existing only between a man and a woman? Probably because we have been conditioned to do so by countless love stories in books, films, plays and on television. Down through history there have been endless accounts of "star-crossed lovers" destined never to share the great love they feel for each other.

But this same love can be expressed in many different guises: between two men, two women, two friends, a brother and sister, a mother and child, etc. It is our earthly consciousness, not our spiritual awareness, that spurs us on to search out the perfect partner. This is nature pushing us to procreate—a purely physical urge that we share with the animals.

Today, many imperfect and unpleasant family relationships exist as a result of people choosing a mate solely on the basis of physical attraction, without any sort of spiritual affinity between the two souls. Irresponsible parenting, child abuse, unhappiness and neglect are all too often the results of such marriages. Parents may feel little or no love for their children because there is no karmic tie; husbands and wives fall out of love with each other once the initial excitement of the marriage wears off, because there is no spiritual bond.

Sometimes a soul needs to reincarnate but can find no clear way to join itself with previous karmic ties, so in its desperation it will choose to enter the womb of a mother with whom it has no prior spiritual bond. Such a situation can alienate the child from its parents, and eventually the child will separate itself from them and go off into the world on its own, seeking its own way and its own relationships, looking for karmic ties with others. This can cause a great deal of pain and anguish in families, as the true cause remains unknown.

The essence of life is love; it must be understood and experienced in all its different forms if the soul is to progress and grow. Concern and understanding for all mankind is a part of this love. As love begins with the Almighty and descends into nature in the form of male-female attraction, it must be recognized and appreciated in all its facets of expression. Love of life and of humanity brings us straight to love of all nature and of God. Our love must be extended to all types of relationships. We should not be selective and stingy with our love, but rather offer it to all the world, to all those in need.

CHAPTER 2

# KARMIC MEDITATION

We all have problems, difficulties to confront in every area of our lives: relationships, emotions, careers, childhood, business, addiction—these are only a few of the subjects that cause stress and unhappiness. This book offers a new beginning—a place to start to eliminate fear and insecurity from your life. When you come to understand the part karma plays in your life, you will begin to understand who you are and why you do the things you do.

The following techniques can be utilized while you are at home, working in the office, on the subway, driving through traffic—almost anytime.

You begin in a very simple manner: take a pad of paper and a pencil. Head it with today's date. Then make a list of everything you can think of that is blocking your happiness. Include everything and everyone—be as complete as possible. Take your time—if it takes several days to complete the task, that doesn't matter. What's important is being as thorough as possible.

If you are one of those rare individuals who can find nothing to put on your list, then this book is not for you. You are indeed blessed.

## PREPARING FOR MEDITATION

The key to discovering your karmic intention in this life is meditation. Thrugh Karmic Meditation you can learn how to direct yourself to the desired esoteric level of awareness, according to your purpose.

You can prepare for meditation as you go through your normal daily routine. But to think that you can change your regular everyday thinking process by preparing for only ten or fifteen minutes is like trying to run a two-minute mile after only a ten-minute warmup! It is virtually impossible to reach the higher levels of consciousness without the correct preparation procedures. Many would-be meditators fall asleep during the process, overtired and completely unprepared for the experience of meditation.

The process of meditation can be rather complex and should not be undertaken lightly. It is essential to know *why* you are contemplating meditation. What is your purpose? What are your goals? Turning off the TV and lighting a candle is not enough.

As each new day begins, people all over the world get out of bed and stagger off into their day. Taking a fresh approach to the ordinary and directing your thought patterns to an alternate energy flow will allow you to start your day right.

## ORGANIZING YOUR THINKING

When you begin your day in light and appreciation, you are beginning to organize your thinking process. You are beginning to gain control of your life instead of merely reacting to everything that happens to you. Changing your normal thought process and feeling in total control of yourself gives you a wonderful new start.

The first step is to set aside a special time and place where you can be totally alone. Here you can approach meditation on a very personal level. Ideally, you should have a separate room set aside for meditating. I realize that this is not always possible, but as long as you have some area where you can be by yourself, you can create your own peaceful retreat. Having a special area just for your Karmic Meditation will help your busy mind relax and enable you to concentrate fully on your purpose. Using this same area repeatedly creates an organized pattern of behavior which will make your meditation easier and easier the more you practice it.

## CREATING YOUR MEDITATION AREA

If you don't have a separate room at your disposal, rearrange your bedroom to create a corner used only for meditation. If your household is a busy one, perhaps a corner of the garage will do. You can even use the bathroom if all else fails.

Creating your meditation area should be a very enjoyable experience. Whatever you feel appropriate to include there is right for you. The amount of space you have available will help you decide what you need.

Your first priority will be to determine what position you wish to meditate in. You may prefer to lie on a soft rug or cot, or you may wish to sit in a comfortable chair or on a meditation cushion. Wherever you are and whatever your position, you should be comfortable. If you are not comfortable, no matter how exotic your area, you will not be able to concentrate on meditating.

However, let me caution you against getting too comfortable. It is all too easy to drift off to sleep if you are overly relaxed and not used to meditating. For this reason I don't recommend lying on your bed to meditate.

If you go into any home you recognize a definite style of decoration. You see objects and furnishings that are a part of the occupant's taste. Some you may like, others may not be to your taste. In "furnishing" your meditation area, colors, fabrics, incense, candles, etc., are all a part of your personal taste. The purpose of creating your own meditation area is to have the ideal surroundings for your own personal sensitivities. This place should reflect you and only you. You should strive to create ideal surroundings, where you can forget the details and stress of your busy life and relax totally. Whatever makes you feel at peace is exactly what you should include in your area.

Music can play a large role in calming the busy mind. Here again, your choice of music must be appealing to you and not obtrusive. When purchasing a tape or record, listen to it before you buy it, if possible.

Naturally, the amount of space you have available will determine the furnishings in your area. I recommend that you include a small table or stool to use for holding a candle, incense, crystal, book or anything else you may need.

Color is also important. Plain white walls are easy to work with, but beware of excess color and decoration. Too much can interfere with your mood and purpose for meditation. Your decor should be peaceful and harmonious, to make you feel comfortable and relaxed.

Whether your area is colorful and exciting or as austere as a monk's cell, you should allow your Higher Self to select the items in it. You may find that you already have exactly what you need in your home, and that when they are arranged suitably, they create the perfect meditation area for you.

## DRESSING FOR MEDITATION

Coming home from work or school and trying to meditate in coat and tie or hose and heels will not work! Make it a point to change into clothing that is loose and comfortable before beginning your meditation. It's very important to remove the clothes you have worn all day, as the vibrations from the outside world cling to them for quite some time and can be very negative.

Your choice of meditation garments is as entirely personal as your surroundings. You may find a colorful robe to your liking, or simply a loose white gown. A full nightgown or comfortable sweats are ideal. Whatever you choose, selecting a garment that is used only for meditation is preferable.

Before you put on your meditation garment, I recommend that you bathe. Cleansing the body removes existing negative vibrations and exhilarates the aura. Long hair should be worn up so that the chakra at the neck can function properly. Feet should be bare, or use comfortable sandals or slippers which expose the toes. If your feet are cold, socks may be worn, preferably woolen ones.

All costume jewelry should be removed. Precious metals, such as gold or silver, may remain unless you associate the pieces with negative situations or relationships. Other objects which might distract or annoy you, such as watches, glasses, hairpins or belts, should be removed also.

You may prefer to wear nothing at all, and this is perfectly all right, providing the room temperature is agreeable to you.

## CHECKLIST FOR MEDITATION

Here's a final checklist to use before beginning your meditation:

1. Choose a time for your daily meditation and try to do it this same time each day. Bedtime is not a good time, as you may

be tired and unable to concentrate. You should not be physically tired, but alert and ready to learn, for meditation is an educational process.

2. Remove your street clothes and take a warm, relaxing bath or shower. Don't rush yourself.

3. Put on your meditation garment.

4. Ensure that you won't be disturbed by locking the door, attending to pets and/or children and making sure that your telephone or answering machine won't bother you.

5. If you wish to light a candle or candles, make sure that they are lit and in a safe place before you begin to meditate. If you don't have nondrip candles, then prepare a holder for the wax to drip into.

6. If you wish to burn incense (a good idea), make sure it is burning properly before meditating. Remember that if you have only a small area at your disposal, incense can become very powerful, perhaps too strong, so take this into consideration.

7. You may wish to record the directions for the meditation procedures.* This will help you to follow along without having to learn each meditation step by step. Those of you who belong to a meditation group will find that playing a tape with the step-by-step procedures will assist everyone in the group meditation.

8. Before commencing, decide exactly which meditations you are going to do. Otherwise, you will find yourself unfocused and inclined to drift away into a state of semi-sleep.

In Chapter 4 I will give you the first in a series of Karmic Meditations that you will encounter throughout this book. There are 22 of them, and you will find that some are based on seven of the Major Arcana in the Connolly Tarot, published here for the first time. Other meditations deal with your Guardian Angel, the Tree of Life, relationships, letting go of pain, your chakras and other esoteric areas.

But before we begin these actual Karmic Meditations, let's look at some preparatory Esoteric Exercises you can do first thing in the morning and throughout the day to help prepare yourself for meditation later on.

*See Appendix for details of recording meditations.

# CHAPTER 3

# ESOTERIC EXERCISES

Immediately after you wake in the morning, even before you open your eyes, you can begin the first of several Esoteric Exercises that will energize and refresh you. Your day will go more smoothly and you will be preparing yourself for your evening meditation as you go about your daily chores.

## EXERCISE 1: STARTING YOUR DAY

With your eyes still closed, visualize a beautiful WHITE light around you. Feel this WHITE light fill up your bedroom, your whole house. Bring the WHITE light down through the top of your head and through your body, forming a bright ball of light beneath your feet. Inhale slowly one deep breath of WHITE light. Let it circulate throughout your body. As you exhale and release the light, feel the energy clearing, cleansing and energizing every inch of your head and body. Feel all levels of consciousness being penetrated by this morning blessing. In joy and appreciation, give thanks.

When time is short, instead of worrying about what the day has in store for you, smile and say Thank you. You can say one big THANK YOU or a lot of little individual thank you's, such as:

THANK YOU FOR THOSE WHO LOVE ME.

THANK YOU FOR MY HEALTH.

THANK YOU FOR MY LIFE.

THANK YOU FOR MY HOME.

13

THANK YOU FOR MY FAMILY.
THANK YOU FOR MY WORK.
THANK YOU FOR BEING WITH ME.

It's not necessary to take any more time than normal. While comb-ing your hair—give thanks. While taking your shower—give thanks. While putting on your clothes—give thanks. While drinking your coffee—give thanks. While getting in your car—give thanks.

Now you are ready to start your day. Every cell in your body has been refreshed and energized. You'll find that your mornings will go much better, for you will be employing the total reverse of your usual thinking process. Instead of reacting negatively to everything that may occur, you start to project the energy you brought in when you woke up. This vitalizing energy will fill your aura, protect you from exter-nal negativity and clear your mind. You'll be able to think more clearly, and consequently your day will go much better.

It takes only one breath to fill your car with WHITE light as you drive to work or school. Don't succumb to worry or anger the minute you hit the road. Look around you and give thanks:

THANK YOU FOR THIS WONDERFUL MORNING.
THANK YOU FOR THE OPPORTUNITIES AHEAD.
THANK YOU FOR CARING ABOUT ME.
THANK YOU FOR ALL THE COMFORTS IN LIFE.
THANK YOU FOR THE STRENGTH TO MEET MY OBLIGA-TIONS.
THANK YOU FOR BEING WITH ME THROUGHOUT MY DAY.

## EXERCISE 2: KEEPING THE LINE OPEN THROUGHOUT THE DAY

Meditation is a way of life. Continuity is important! During the day you should remember to keep the line to the light open. I don't mean that you should disappear into the restroom every half hour to chant an affirmation. There's a much easier method of keeping your esoteric line open no matter how busy you are during the day.

After beginning with the first Esoteric Exercise and giving thanks for all your blessings, your next step is to allow your Higher Consciousness to develop while you are busy using your conscious mind elsewhere.

Here is a simple but effective procedure that you can use throughout the day.

Inform yourself that you will be projecting BLUE light at regular intervals during your workday. Once you have done this, your Higher Self will take over.

The color BLUE you will be using is a deep, beautiful COBALT. This intense BLUE has the esoteric power to heal on all levels—mental, physical and spiritual. The recipient feels extremely good when receiving this BLUE healing light.

There are only two steps to this exercise:

1. Breathe IN WHITE light.
2. Breathe OUT BLUE light.

It takes only one breath and you can give so much. Imagine yourself walking through your office or place of business. You see a fellow employee hard at work at a nearby desk. Perhaps he or she seems tired or restless. Breathe in WHITE light; then, looking at that person, exhale BLUE light. Visualize the beam of BLUE light enveloping the person. The energy you project will find its own level and operate where it is needed in that person's aura.

It takes only a second and one breath to help someone feel better. Just think how many breaths you take in one day! By consciously directing only ten, you will be giving of yourself from a higher level, and the recipient will absorb the beautiful and refreshing energy on the level needed at that time.

It takes only ten breaths a day to keep yourself spiritually attuned. The purpose of this exercise is to benefit others, and thereby benefit yourself. "As you give, so you receive." Directing BLUE light to another person is not a demonstrative exercise. No one else will know when you are doing it. If you wish, try it first before a mirror. Inhale WHITE; exhale BLUE. It's as simple as that!

If someone catches you looking at them, just smile as you project the healing BLUE light. It will only add to your esoteric growth. You may wish to give someone more than one healing breath during the day. This is fine also. Once you begin this wonderful daily exercise of giving light to others, you will find much light, both WHITE and BLUE, sustaining your own life path.

Here are a few likely candidates for your healing breaths as you go through the day:

1. A person walking along the sidewalk as you drive by
2. A salesperson in a store
3. A child playing
4. Someone eating in the same restaurant
5. A hospital, as you pass by
6. The family in a house as you fly overhead in an airplane
7. A waitress in a coffee shop
8. The attendant at a gas station
9. The mailman
10. A school
11. Your boss or supervisor; your employee
12. A family member leaving the house
13. Anyone who looks ill or lonely or homeless.

Projecting light to a sleeping person is ideal, for during sleep the various levels of consciousness are more relaxed. Therefore, the energy you send will have a more profound impact.

This esoteric activity will enhance the power of your Karmic Meditations. You will experience a greater continuity of thought and application and become less self-centered after sharing this healing gift with others. By keeping your spiritual line open throughout each day, you will find it easier to attain the correct level for meditation and reduce the stress in your life.

## STRESS AWARENESS

"Stress" is another word for pressure. Stress occurs when certain areas of your life become vulnerable to outside pressures. These influences may be self-instigated or come from other people and situations. Stress can be found in any aspect of human nature. It is usually first felt on the emotional level. Stress can also affect your general health. Your thinking process becomes restricted, and soon you are affected mentally, physically and spiritually.

When stress is focused on one particular area, it is easier to analyze. The cause is usually obvious, and a plan of action can be conceived to eliminate the stress by dealing directly with the cause.

General stress, however, is more complex and difficult to isolate. Many people suffer from this kind of stress: a little pressure here and a little pressure there soon amounts to pressure everywhere. Eventually it grows to the point where you begin to notice it, but you feel you can handle it. However, after awhile it begins to affect you physically. At this point you see your doctor, who prescribes, and you submit, attempting to live and cope with constant chaos in your life.

General stress, which spreads out into all areas of your life, is the worst form of this ailment. As one area is being treated, another is being afflicted. There seems to be no way out!

Well, I'm here to tell you that there *is* a way out, but it requires your fullest cooperation to make it work. The following Esoteric Exercise will help you discover a way to begin to rid yourself of the Stress Monster.

All you need for this exercise are five blank sheets of paper, a pencil and a willingness to be honest with yourself.

## EXERCISE 3: STRESS ANALYSIS

Choose a time and place where you will not be disturbed. Relax your mind and body for a few minutes. Let your mind flow backward into the past, as you return to the beginning of your problems.

### Sheet 1: How It All Began

Being as honest and thorough as possible, write down all the facts and incidents you can recall that might have brought on the stress. Use dates whenever you can. Mention the people involved, places, times— anything you can think of that might be relevant. Number each item consecutively. If you simply cannot recall the beginning, you might want to skip ahead to Chapter 4 and do Karmic Meditations 1 and 2, to help bring forgotten causes and origins into consciousness.

### Sheet 2: The Direction Taken, Step by Step

Using numbers, begin with the first step you took and list all the steps that led you in the direction you have gone. List them as concisely but as completely as possible. Keep each individual step separate from the others. Do not try to judge your past actions or justify them. Do not modify or change the true circumstances. You are trying to determine *how* the stress developed.

## Sheet 3: Casualty Sheet

On this sheet write down the effect of each step on Sheet 2, using the same numbering system to identify cause and effect. List the effect without emotion—good, bad or indifferent. Make your report as objective and factual as you can. Remember, you are a war correspondent here! Don't list blame or try to judge the result of the effect.

## Sheet 4: What Should Have Been Done

This is a tough sheet to complete! Don't be too hard on yourself here. It may or may not have been possible for you to act according to what you list on this sheet. Simply put down what you feel you should have done in each situation, instead of what you actually did. Be as complete and honest as possible with this list.

It's quite normal to be cynical when working on Sheet 4; as you know, it's so easy to write what should have been done—after you've done something else! In reality, you obviously encountered some difficulties or you would have done the right thing, instead of whatever you did do.

## Sheet 5: Rescue Sheet

This list will take some time to complete. At this point in the exercise, revision is necesssary. Go back and check each point on each sheet. Each step or statement should be numbered to correspond with one another. Look carefully at Number 1 on each sheet and determine how you can rescue the situation as you complete each step. Don't attempt to complete this sheet if you're feeling emotional or tired—you need a clear, objective mind to come up with steps which can tell you plainly and precisely what action to take next to extricate yourself from your stressful situation. Ignore any thoughts that suggest that your Rescue Sheet involves more stress! What it does require is determination, courage and inner strength. With these qualities, you will be well on your way to healing yourself and able to go forward.

Don't write down anything you know is impossible for you—be realistic and objective. Your goal is to rid yourself of stress in all areas. With a sensible, custom-made program of activity, YOU CAN DO IT!

Exercise 3 can be considered complete only when each phase has been satisfactorily worked out. Remember, if you have difficulty beginning, go forward to Meditations 1 or 2 in the next chapter. The remaining steps should be comparatively easy once you have established HOW IT ALL BEGAN.

## EXERCISE 4:  THE ROOT OF STRESS

This fourth Esoteric Exercise requires a certain amount of preparation, without which you will not be able to get to the root of your stress.

Begin with pencil and paper and go back to the beginning. Thanks to the preceding exercise, some of you may now be able to go directly to the source of your stress. Don't worry if you can't. This exercise is to help you not only reach the source but to understand it as well.

If possible, use dates (even approximate dates), as this will help your conscious mind probe as far as possible, at which point your Higher Self will take over and release the necessary information. You should be aware that the nature of your present problem may appear to be totally unrelated to the origin you uncover. Try not to link circumstances like beads on a chain, in order to force things to come together. Just allow your normal thinking process to take you back as far as possible to the source of your stress.

Keep in mind that the true source could have occurred just last week—or even yesterday! If that is so, you won't need this exercise. But in most cases the stress origin will be buried far enough in the past to need discovering and bringing to light.

Remain objective as you write down any glimmers of memory or insight, using pencil and paper. Don't be concerned about too much detail. Esoteric Exercise 1 will have arranged everything in order without causing you distress. Going back to painful situations may be uncomfortable, but not necessarily. Once you have located the source or origin of your dilemma, you need not dwell upon the unhappy details.

If you've decided that you simply can't pinpoint the origin of your stress, then obviously it goes a long way back—probably to a previous lifetime. The key to this exercise is control. Don't allow yourself to try and determine why certain things turned out the way they did, or why you took certain actions instead of others. Keep your determination to be honest, thorough and objective, to stir your present consciousness to go directly to the stress origin. Your present level of consciousness has the ability to cover up deep and distressing events in your past, although it cannot eliminate the memory patterns.

When you have written as much as you can, you will be ready to go on to actual Karmic Meditation. I will give you three more Esoteric Exercises later on in this book, but now it is time for you to consider a very comforting fact: Although you may feel you are all alone in this difficult task of exploring your past, there is a Presence which is always with you, helping you in many spiritual ways. In the following chapter, we will explore this spiritual companion and the ways in which it can assist you in all your endeavors—physical, mental and spiritual.

# CHAPTER 4

# THE SPIRITUAL GUIDE IN MEDITATION

From our ancient beginnings we have consistently used guided imagery in our spiritual endeavors. This is a technique used to elevate the normal level of consciousness. Through the art of visualization we are able to lift ourselves up from our normal thinking process and reach a higher level, projecting a spiritual image. This image is the vehicle for spiritual exploration and wisdom.

## A SPIRITUAL COMPANION

The visualized image is thought of as a living entity on another plane of existence, a separate consciousness embodying the collective knowledge of the universe. The image can be thought of as any of the following:

Master
Spiritual Guide
Guardian Angel
Saint
Spirit of a loved one who has died
Spirit of a companion or lover from a past life.

Once your mind has accepted the possibility of spiritual contact, it establishes a desire for it. This desire is fostered through prayer and other spiritual endeavors. The spiritual companion provides an image for your mind to project from, allowing access to exploration of the outer realms of existence.

21

This companion has the esoteric ability to channel all pertinent information regarding your life path. Special souls elect to do this work and serve as a liaison between man and the love of God.

Many people are privileged to actually see the image of their companion in their meditations, recognizing not only the purpose but the origin of this spiritual relationship. Others accept the existence of a spiritual guide without visual confirmation, knowing intuitively that they have an entity who watches over them, protecting and advising. This entity then becomes the link which connects a person to a vast area of spiritual exploration.

There are many people who cannot accept the idea of a spiritual advisor. For them, the entity must work without their knowledge or acceptance, which makes the task much more difficult. But for those who realize that such companions exist, communication with them and the receiving of knowledge not otherwise accessible becomes a blessed routine.

## ACCEPTING YOUR MASTER

If you have never had this kind of spiritual experience, you can develop your esoteric abilities through meditation. This will bring you into eventual contact with your guide, or your personal spiritual Master. Think of this being as a wise, benevolent teacher whose experience is far beyond your own and whose desire is to help you in whatever way is possible. For many he will be Jesus Christ.

The result of this spiritual link will bring you comfort and strength and a great sense of personal achievement. Meditation can of course be practiced without the assistance of a Master or guide, but the presence of such a companion can greatly accelerate your esoteric learning. By availing yourself of the spiritual help that is so freely offered, you can catapult your receptivity far beyond the limits of everyday consciousness.

All you need do is accept the fact that your Master is available and ready to help you at any time. You must be ready to recognize this fully. You must express your desire for help through prayer and inner belief. Ask that your mind and heart be opened; ask that your Master be present in your meditations, and soon you will feel that presence.

The strength and wisdom of the Master is yours to share. From the Master level you can link yourself to the Christ Consciousness via your belief system, and so on until you reach the God Consciousness Itself.

To begin, firmly establish that you are now in the process of making contact with your Master. Look for subtle signs in your everyday life. Ask that your mind be opened to recognition while you sleep. Use the following meditations and soon you will come to know your personal Master. The joy that results from this recognition is immeasurable. From this point of personal effort you begin your own spiritual development.

Our karmic goals are imprinted on our souls, but the conscious mind is separated from this awareness, creating a gap between what is and what could be. Recognizing your spiritual companion and developing the ability to communicate with this being eliminates the gap and the fear it creates. Trusting in the love and guidance of your Master is the first step in reducing Karmic Stress.

## MEDITATION 1: THE GUARDIAN ANGEL

1. To prepare for this first Karmic Meditation, you must have completed Esoteric Exercise 3, described in Chapter 3. Have Sheet 1 with you, for the material you receive in this meditation will relate to HOW IT ALL BEGAN.

2. Focus on your Inner Eye, which is located just above your nose, between the eyebrows. Slowly inhale a deep breath of warm PINK light. As you exhale, retain the PINK within you and let out GRAY light. As the GRAY is released, feel all negativity—known and unknown, seen and unseen—leaving every part of your mind, body and soul. This breathing procedure is not only important during the meditation but is extremely beneficial in every way at any time. Continue to breathe in and out in this manner until you reach a state of complete relaxation and exerience a deep sense of readiness to proceed.

3. You are now filled with the warmth and protection of the PINK light. You are fully relaxed and have made a conscious effort to release all existing negativity with every GRAY breath. Now, feeling wrapped up in and protected by vibrant PINK energy,

visualize your GUARDIAN ANGEL. This beautiful angel is dressed entirely in many shades of PINK. The purpose of this angel is to protect you at all times from anything that might penetrate your emotional level to such an extent that it could harm your present life path. Although your Guardian Angel performs this duty, it must allow you to experience your own destiny as you originally chose it before this life. Consequently, you are not always aware of the angel's presence. Even though unpleasant things may befall you, the angel remains with you throughout your life, protecting you in thousands of ways that you are never conscious of and eliminating those situations which are not a part of your destiny.

4. Allow your Guardian Angel to manifest fully. Concentrate with your Inner Eye and see your angel in as much detail as possible, surrounded by vibrant PINK light. Feel the desire to merge with the Guardian Angel. Step forward into the warmth of the PINK energy.

5. Visualize your angel with arms outstretched, eager to receive you. Ask for your angel's name.

6. If necessary, wait. Be patient. You will receive the name.

7. Once you hear the angel's name, step forward and hold the angel's hands, saying: [Angel's name], I ASK THAT WITHIN YOUR LOVING PROTECTION YOU RELEASE TO ME THE SOURCE OF MY PRESENT STRESS. Now wait for your answer.

8. When the original source of your Karmic Stress is given, listen carefully. Some of you may experience it as a vision; others may hear it revealed in words. On this level you will have no emotional reaction to the information, for you are well protected here.

9. Immediately after you have been given the source, inhale a deep PINK breath. Slowly release this breath, only this time as PINK light, not GRAY. Thank your Guardian Angel for revealing the source you sought.

10. Hold the knowledge you have received in your mind. Continue to breathe PINK in and out. See the angel and the PINK light permeating everything gradually disappear.

11. Now stretch out and relax for a few moments. Visualize your arms and legs bathed in WHITE light.

12. When you feel ready, open your eyes and write down the information presented to you on Sheet 1: HOW IT ALL BEGAN.

The Guardian Angel meditation helps considerably when you need to probe childhood memories. Both this meditation and the one that follows are very helpful in clearing up past stress. You may enjoy using #1 and then following up with #2. The Master's Bench is also therapeutic; information received on this level is usually quite clear and objective.

## MEDITATION 2:  THE MASTER'S BENCH

This meditation is used to focus into your beginnings. If there is no desire to recall these memories, they may have been filed away deliberately in a "confidential" area of your mind that needs a code for access. This meditation can provide that access code.

Choose a day when everything has gone smoothly. You must be fully relaxed and comfortable, as this meditation requires your full concentration.

1. Relax completely and focus on your Inner Eye. Visualize WHITE light and project it outward, like a beacon. Ask for your MASTER to come. Then wait for your Master to appear at the end of the light beam you have projected. This may be your Guardian Angel.

2. When your Master appears, show your appreciation by giving thanks for the appearance. Ask for your Master's name.

3. Step forward into the WHITE light beam and walk toward your Master. The WHITE energy is very strong, so don't be put off if you feel a resisting force. Continue to walk forward. When you reach your Master, reach out with your arms and feel your Master take hold of your hands.

4. Now visualize a beautiful GREEN forest all around you. The peaceful GREEN vibrations begin over your Master's head. See them flow down to color the Master's robe. Feel yourself become completely saturated with this beautiful GREEN energy.

5. Walk with your Master to the Master's Bench and sit down. Be aware of the many paths around this bench. Lower your head and, thinking clearly, feel WHITE light encompass you and your Master.

6. When the WHITE light has completely dispersed the GREEN, ask your Master to show you the beginnings of your stress— HOW IT ALL BEGAN.

7. If your need is sincere your Master will show approval with a smile or a nod of the head. As your Master begins to walk, follow the path chosen.

8. As you walk, look straight at your Master. When there is something for you to see, your Master will point it out to you. Watch everything with interest, for you are being taken back to the beginning. The images you see along the path are essential to your understanding.

9. Take your time and absorb the information being presented. Avoid becoming emotional, for this will remove you from the meditation level. When you have the information you need, and it seems clear to you, reach out your hands and feel the color GREEN surround you again. Feel the tranquility of knowledge and call for your Master. Your Master will be in the GREEN vibrations. Greet your Master and follow back to the Master's Bench. Sit and hold your Master's hands.

10. Feel the strong power of the WHITE light again and ask your Master any questions you may have.

11. When you are ready to return, your Master will lead you back through your original WHITE beam. Thank your Master for the information you have been given. Feel yourself moving forward until you merge back into the WHITE energy of your Inner Eye.

12. Relax and slowly count to SEVEN. Then open your eyes and write down every detail of what you have experienced on Sheet 1: HOW IT ALL BEGAN.

CHAPTER 5

# INVOLUNTARY FOCUS

When for no apparent reason you find yourself thinking about a particular situation, person, place or period of time in history, your mind is demonstrating what I like to call INVOLUNTARY FOCUS. Apparently, when the conscious mind is relaxed, the Higher Consciousness submits information stored in its memory banks to the conscious mind, information which is somehow relevant to present circumstances.

It might be that during the process of your daily duties your conscious mind recognized a karmic factor that would have some meaning for you. But you were busy concentrating on other things at the time, so your mind conveniently stored the information for later. Later, when you were relaxed, your Higher Self picked up this information and released it as significant data for you to decipher. Often this valuable information is discarded as being strange, nonsensical, irrelevant— merely daydreams.

For example, a particular person you see or meet might arouse memories of a past relationship, but you might think, "I feel that I know this person, but if so, why don't I remember him?" The answer can be quite complex. First of all, if this person was known to you in a previous life, his physical appearance now will be totally different. Your Higher Self recognizes the soul vibrations, although your conscious mind does not. The same goes for situations, places and periods of history.

Visiting a foreign country, reading a particular book, hearing a certain kind of music—such experiences can arouse the Akashic memory bank in your mind. If the connection is of particular importance, you will feel a continuous urge to return to the place, or at least read more about it—to investigate more fully what is calling to you. Your conscious mind is putting up a barrier against this knowledge as it goes about the business of dealing with mundane affairs, but here is where Karmic Mediation comes into play!

## INVOLUNTARY FOCUS AND *DÉJÀ VU*

Involuntary Focus is a key to discovering past-life events that correlate with present-life circumstances. This feeling of having experienced something before, or been a certain place before, is known as *déjà vu*, as mentioned briefly in Chapter 1. Involuntary Focus can be considered a continuation or elaboration of *déjà vu* if it is encouraged and investigated.

The secret to using the sense of *déjà vu* for your karmic benefit is to concentrate on the visual memory as strongly as possible, lock it tightly in your mind until you are able to investigate it further. Capture the essence of the person, place or situation and hold it until you can concentrate on it fully and apply your Karmic Meditation.

Don't discard your *déjà vu* impressions merely because they seem difficult to understand, odd or irrelevant. Whatever the situation, trust your Higher Self to know what it's doing and accept the feeling as something that is important to you.

## INVOLUNTARY FOCUS AND RELATIONSHIPS

*Déjà vu* is not the only avenue of Involuntary Focus. You may find that you have a strong feeling toward a particular country or race of people throughout your life. This may be something your conscious mind can't explain, since you may never have visited this country, nor had much contact with the people who seem to attract you. You might have a desire to live in a particular house, or style of house, with a fixation on certain types of furnishings.

Involuntary Focus can be triggered by a glance, a casual word, a fragrance. Once you realize that your present level of consciousness cannot explain your interest, you have every chance of learning how to discover why this occurs.

To investigate through Karmic Meditation can unfold and reveal vital memory patterns that pertain to your present life. For example, you might discover that your present spouse was your parent in a former life. Your present child might have been your sister or brother. This can explain many present-day relationship patterns that you are now experiencing or have experienced in the past.

Your probe or investigation must commence at the source, which is the Higher Self. The minute you begin the investigation at the present level of consciousness, you are going in the opposite direction from exploring the Involuntary Focus.

Your present level of consciousness does not always find it easy to accept that there is vital information locked in a higher level of consciousness. Also, it may have difficulty accepting that your child may have been your wife, husband, brother, sister or even parent in a past life.

What could be the reason or purpose for this, you may ask. The answer is to fulfill the soul on varying levels of life experience. The relationship of a husband and wife is not identical to that of a brother and sister or parent and child. We give to each other, and love each other according to the relationships we have. Therefore, an alternate relationship gives us a chance to experience other methods of expression and responsibility. How we interact with one another is how we develop our soul's evolution here on earth.

A good example of how karma is developed according to past-life relationships can be seen in my novel, *Earthdance* (Newcastle, 1984). In this story we see eleven people deal with various relationships among one another through several lifetimes. Each experience determines the next. Each relationship is explored in another, yet the journey of the soul is clear.

Involuntary Focus is a tool that can be used to understand where you are on the path of lives. There always will be relationships that need nurturing, obligations to be fulfilled and of course karmic debts to be paid to others. In this fascinating area of study you find that you can go beyond your previous restrictions. Once the Higher Self begins to release knowledge to the conscious level, you discover how vast and magnificent life after life really is.

What is really exciting is that you can have access to this knowledge! As with any other learning procedure, it takes time and patience. But the results are extraordinarily rewarding and available to anyone who has a true desire to learn more about their own lifepath.

Working with Involuntary Focus is developing the seed that your Higher Self feels is necessary for you at this point in your life. To ignore this is to close the doors to your higher wisdom. Unlock these doors and you will discover the hitherto unknown possibilities of hidden talents and abilities. Have you ever experienced an urge to express yourself in a different way? Do you feel that you have the ability to be artistic? to write books or music? Reach the source of this silent urge by capturing the message of Involuntary Focus.

## MEDITATION 3:  THE ARCHWAY

After preliminary preparation for meditation:

1. Write down exactly what created your Involuntary Focus. Be as concise as possible, but also as accurate as possible.

2. Lie down quietly and review in your mind what you have written about the circumstances surrounding the Involuntary Focus. Add any details that you may have overlooked.

3. Focus your attention on the top center of your head. In this area visualize a bright WHITE light, half an inch in diameter.

4. Take your time and breathe easily. With each breath you inhale, visualize the WHITE light entering your Inner Eye; then HOLD the breath for a moment.

5. Release the WHITE light through the top center of your head. Each time you do this, the bright WHITE light expands.

6. Remember to hold the breath for a moment before releasing it. This procedure will stimulate the Crown Chakra and enhance the purpose of this meditation. As you continue the exercise, the WHITE energy expands in size from the original half inch to a full OPEN CROWN of WHITE light.

7. At this point in your meditation visualize the WHITE light as a crown over the top of your head. Now *immediately* turn

your attention to a glowing disc of WHITE energy directly in the center of your body (the Umbilical Chakra, located two or three inches above the navel).

8. Now start to breathe and move in the WHITE energy up through the Umbilical Chakra. As you inhale, feel the light rise UP, UP, UP to the Crown Chakra and release accordingly.

9. Continue this procedure and feel your inner self rising with your breath to the Crown Chakra. Feel your desire to be released and go to the Archway of Past Experience.

10. Allow the urge to push you up; look ahead of you. Now see the Archway and see your Master.

11. Your Master knows your purpose. Walk through the Archway with your Master and LISTEN, OBSERVE and ENJOY.

12. When your experience is finished, your Master will bring you back to the Archway. You will see a strong WHITE light. Enter this light.

13. Breathe in deeply through the Inner Eye and exhale DOWN into your physical body. Do this THREE TIMES and lie still.

14. Contemplate your spiritual experience. Recognize how good your physical body feels and GIVE THANKS.

15. After contemplation, open your eyes and IMMEDIATELY WRITE DOWN your experience.

Like all meditation exercises, this one requires constant practice. You may have your first spiritual experience the first time you reach the Archway. On the other hand, you may need to go through the Archway with your Guide several times. Regardless of what knowledge you bring back to your conscious level, each visitation is a wonderful and uplifting spiritual adventure. Enjoy it.

CHAPTER 6

# UNDERSTANDING KARMIC RELATIONSHIPS

As we look deeper into the mysteries of karma and reincarnation, eventually we will be forced to look at the many nations of the world where people live at a level of poverty that is almost unbearable to consider. Pestilence, famine and violence is all some souls will ever experience; they will be lucky (or perhaps not so lucky!) to live through such terrible and inhuman conditions.

Who are these souls? Are they being severely punished for past transgressions? There is more than one answer to these important questions.

## KARMA AND MOTHERHOOD

A woman yields to her karmic desires and responsibilities when she receives the initial urge to become pregnant. We cannot ignore the many births that are unplanned and unwanted. Each soul is driven by the need for rebirth to continue its personal pattern of growth and self-expressions. It is not always possible to be born into the desired circumstances, but this does not mean that if a soul cannot complete its destiny in a given life, it must be born into an undesirable family environment.

But many souls deliberately elect to be born into terrible and inhuman circumstances. Their purpose in doing this is to alert the world to these conditions and to do what they can to ensure that misery and starvation will eventually be overcome. Many new leaders will emerge

32

from the impoverished nations as a result of the higher souls who will eventually correct these conditions through education and enlightened leadership.

When a woman senses the desire to give birth, she is actually receiving contact from a soul who requires birth. To attract a soul who is an important part of her karmic intent, the woman should prepare herself well before the baby is born.

The incoming soul is very definitely attracted to the mother's aura. Each aura has its own individual vibratory rate. The mother's aura can become more attractive to the soul if she concentrates on its beauty. How the mother thinks and feels contributes to her aura and establishes a vibratory force field which will attract the energy of a familiar and loving soul. By the same token, a depleted aura can repel the proper soul. If the pregnant woman thinks only of her own problems and pains, her selfishness reduces the vibratory force of her aura. Like attracts like; consequently, the mother attracts according to her own personal energy level.

The pregnant mother should respond immediately to her pregnancy with joy and anticipation. This response registers in her own aura, thus extending the vibratory pattern like a lighthouse in a storm. The soul may join its own energy to the mother's aura immediately after she becomes pregnant. She is then able to extend this energy and enlarge her own aura. Generally speaking, it takes approximately four and a half to five months before the soul enters the womb. An extremely old expression refers to this period as the "quickening."

The actual nature of the soul is already established before physical birth. How this nature is expressed can be enhanced by the energy balance of the mother during the pregnancy. We know, for example, that music during pregnancy is very satisfying to the unborn baby. The equilibrium and influence of the mother plays a great part in how the baby initially expresses its own unique personality.

This influence extends into the child's early behavior patterns as it develops. Once the little one is exposed fully to family and friends, it is further influenced. I think of the word "influence" as you might think of a very thin covering or veil. As the child experiences adolescence these veils or influences are removed. The methods of and reasons for removing these influences vary depending on the relationships involved. Some are gently removed, and the adolescent is assisted by the family through this period of growth and change without undue stress. As the young person reaches maturity, they are able to recognize their potential and develop naturally into a well-balanced adult.

The opposite of this process occurs when the adolescent is unhappy and lacks ambition. Feeling enormous pressures and the need for release, they appear to tear apart all the original foundations, good, bad or indifferent. Such negative behavior patterns expose the family to anger and hurt. The mother, of course, always remains a mother, but the adolescent moves on to experience other roles in life.

Another esoteric aspect of mother and child is the level of sensitivity they are able to share. In a good mother-and-child relationship the mother often knows exactly how her offspring feels in certain circumstances, especially emotional ones. This link can also be formed between father and child, depending on the family situation.

A level of sensitivity that is absolutely unique develops between mother and child. The mother has the receptive energy and is able to take upon herself the emotional level of her child. This situation is a continuation of their relationship before physical birth. The soul of the child actually can impregnate the mother's aura before conception. During the pregnancy, as the child's aura begins to form, both mother and baby share a joint vibratory force. The father can also participate in this phenomenon if the mother and father are exceptionally close and loving. When both parents are full of joy and anticipation regarding the birth of the baby, they connect with the child's aura. Then, when the baby's aura merges with the mother's, the strength and love of the father is also absorbed.

After the baby is born, as long as there is love there will be this esoteric connection between mother and child. To understand this further, you must consider the aura and its permanent vibratory force. If a child is secure and loved he will feel content with the mother energy around him. This energy merges initially prior to physical birth and becomes a root force in the child's aura. Therefore, when the child is experiencing trouble, his concerns are transmitted into the aura field and touch upon the root energy of the aura. This energy is independent, yet has an esoteric link with the mother.

This link between mother and child has nothing to do with the love they have for each other. It is a separate esoteric tie which appears to grow in strength when there is a bond of love. It becomes less apparent if mother and child become emotionally severed, yet the influence they have on each other remains throughout life. I think of this link as the esoteric umbilical cord.

We know that the father determines the sex of the child. We also know that the mother attracts the soul of the child for whatever purpose. That purpose may be for the soul to connect strongly with the father or someone else, but nevertheless it is through the aura of the mother that the new soul makes its earthly appearance.


## THE NATURE OF LOVE

It could be said that karma is another word for destiny. Karma is the totality of one's acts and deeds in any one of the successive states of one's experiences. Each life is predestined prior to rebirth. The lifepath is mapped out according to the needs of the soul on its journey back to God.

Relationships play a large part in our personal progress. It may be difficult to accept that each life episode could feature the same characters, who for the purpose and direction of individual karma, come together in various relationship patterns. Each person adjusts to a different personality role, much the same way as an actor adapts to each different part in a play.

Consider for a moment why this should be. The complexity of love, which stems from the universe, creates a distinct nature of its own, depending on the type of relationship involved. It is quite natural to feel that various kinds of love each have their own purpose. That may be so, but the overall plan or purpose is for us to learn the power of love in every form. For it is all one and all the same.

When the soul rebirths it would seem that this understanding of universal love is relinquished. Prior to birth the soul has access to this knowledge, but when rebirth occurs it appears to retain only partial wisdom regarding the universal plan.

As we separate from this universal ability, we learn to rely on our emotional level. Once a relationship has been initiated, the information is sifted through the emotional level to determine the nature of our feeling. The term "love" becomes modified and classified according to the type of relationship being established.

There is, for example, parental love; the love between two friends; between brothers and sisters and between man and wife. Essentially, it all comes from the same sourace of universal love. Yet we are capable of feeling love's impact and analyzing its content to make it conform with the accepted terms of relationships here on earth. The emotional level can be activated without warning, causing a normal situation to develop into something special and long-remembered. The emotional level can also provide a protective barrier until further information is entered.

When we try to convey the nature of love, we often define how we feel by saying that we feel "deeply attached" or that our love is "very deep." Once we find ourselves profoundly attached to another, the emotional level provides a buffer or protection. During this period the concentration on the loved one is not challenged until the emotional level accepts all the aspects of this special relationship. Only after familiarity occurs does the conscious level allow us to be critical of the now absorbed emotional bond.

Many relationships are bonded in pain. They are not always evenly balanced. Some relationships appear to be extremely one-sided: one person apparently is the giver and the other is the taker. Yet the relationship remains bonded. In these types of relationships karma is evidently the motivating seed. This kind of union between two people is seldom understood. Say Partners A and B are attracted to each other. After the exciting beginning of the relationship, Partner A feels hurt, mistreated, betrayed and angry. This unhappy state of existence is almost impossible to understand. Taking a karmic view, we would say that Partner A owes Partner B a karmic debt.

That may be so, but Partner A cannot allow the repayment of karma to go on indefinitely! This is where the nucleus of the problem lies, in not knowing *when* the karmic debt has been paid. Clues are presented throughout. When Partner A realizes that he has repaid his debt, life introduces new opportunities. For example, new prospective partners, job and career opportunities or residential changes. Partner A is presented with CHOICES. This is when he can use his free will within his path of destiny. Unfortunately, these options are not always taken; then the relationship can transform into reverse karma! Partner B now begins to create a new karmic debt and now becomes the debtor.

So you can see how this maze of karmic obligations can bring back together undesirable and unnecessary relationships, life after life. After karmic debts are paid, you should realize that your true partner now has the opportunity to be recognized and accepted.

When two souls experience attraction and love followed by pain and severance, one or both partners become reluctant to end the relationship they have established. Often the urge to complete an undesirable relationship is overridden by fear of the unknown, fear of entering another relationship. These people would rather hang on to what they know than explore and discover a new partner. It means starting all over again—going through all the preliminary stages of courtship without knowing for sure whether they are going to be hurt again.

The secret of ending unwanted relationships is to avoid jumping immediately into another romantic situation! The emotional level needs to recuperate and restore its normal balance. When Partner A tells Partner B that it's all over, the emotional level continues to function. This is where the pain of severance is rooted. A person needs to heal and recover their normal emotional balance without the input of a partner who is no longer there. This will take effort. During this time you should concentrate solely on yourself. A great deal of emotion has been absorbed. Mind, body and soul have all undergone great trauma. After a continual focus of energy on another person's behavior, reactions and temperament, it is not easy to REDIRECT these feelings towards yourself. It is a lonely and painful process, and during it you often lose interest in your normal, everyday affairs.

This period of time will not go on forever! If you concentrate on your personal adjustment and new ideas and thoughts regarding your own welfare, the emotional level will begin to function correctly again and your conscious mind will be forced to look in alternative directions. When balanced, the emotional level will respond to new ventures and attractions.

The following Karmic Meditation will help you discover answers and assist you in focusing on and recognizing the bond that holds you. After you have become familiar with the procedure, you will be able to explore your depths and recognize the foundations on which you built this relationship.

## MEDITATION 4: UNDERSTANDING YOUR RELATIONSHIP

Before we begin, let me emphasize certain basic procedures. The practice of this particular meditation arouses deep feelings imbedded in the emotional level. Any emotion expressed during the meditation can be thought of as a release mechanism. The essential point is NOT to begin this meditation unless you are feeling balanced.

This meditation is to help you see clearly exactly what your true feelings are regarding the relationship. From this point you will be able to investigate the seeds of your relationship, which in turn should help you gain a better understanding of it. Because your feelings and emotions are deeply involved with your question, take a little longer to fully relax.

1. You are warm and very comfortable. Visualize yourself lying on a warm, sandy beach.

2. It is still and quiet—you can hear the gulls screeching.

3. This is a beautiful, peaceful feeling. Enjoy this feeling. You are alone, completely alone. A gentle ocean breeze passes over your face.

4. Concentrate on your Inner Eye after the breeze has left you.

5. Easily and gently visualize breathing in through the Inner Eye an invigorating RED energy. Effortlessly allow this RED energy to circulate throughout your entire body, then RELEASE it through your arms and fingers—legs and toes.

6. As you release the breath, feel it emerge from your fingers and toes in vibrant shades of REDS and PINKS.

7. Continue to do this and become aware of the vibrant energy building all around you. It is fortifying your aura, reinforcing your spirituality.

8. Now become the center, the soul center of this magnificent energy. Enjoy this for a moment; you are being renewed and receiving higher energies.

9. All your levels are being strengthened—mental, spiritual and physical. Each intake of breath increases your strength. Each time you exhale you add to the radiance of your aura.

10. When you are ready, get up and walk to the ocean's edge. Feel the sand under your feet. Allow the gentle lap of the waves to touch your toes.

11. As you look at the ocean, see the reflection of the RED sunset dancing on the water.

12. With arms outstretched, breathing easily and normally, look up into the brilliant sky. See the thousands of stars; see the full moon as a huge SILVER sphere in the heavens.

13. Know that you are a part of nature, that all of this is you. Drink in this power and beauty and feel all negativity—known and unknown, seen and unseen—fall away from you.

14. As the negativity leaves you, each incoming wave washes it away. Each breath you inhale releases your deepest negativity and it flows away from you as you exhale.

15. The waves gently come in, forcefully removing all remaining negativity. Be aware of your innter strength; when you are totally free of negativity, look for the path of the moon.

16. In the brilliance of the moonlight you see a path along the shore. Follow this path to the rocks beyond and see your MASTER waiting for you.

17. As you approach your Master, extend your greeting and sit with him or her upon the sand.

18. Say clearly: I NEED TO UNDERSTAND MY RELATION-SHIP WITH [Name the person].

19. You are alone with your Master. You can hear the ocean and see the waves. Relax and allow the Master to reveal wisdom to you. Feel free to talk with your Master and ask questions. You will be told when to return. Empty yourself and ask all you need to know. Allow any remaining emotions to flow freely. From the depths of your being ask and be ready to receive wisdom.

20. You will be shown various situations that are relevant and important regarding your relationship. If you are ready, your Master will give you advice and explain the nature of your relationship, be it good, bad or indifferent.

21. Now you are ready to return. Thank your Master, then say good-bye and walk back the way you came along the edge of the shore. Bathe your feet again in the gentle waves. Look out at the horizon and know that YOU KNOW.

22. Go back to your place on the sand. Lie down and give thanks for the knowledge and understanding received.

23. Relax and contemplate for a while what you have learned. Then open your eyes and make notes of your experience.

This beautiful meditation can be used whenever you feel the need to explore your relationships and find answers. Enjoy it.

CHAPTER 7

# THE KARMIC CROSSROADS

There are many ways in which we can suffer Karmic Stress, and its negative effects may be seen in many ways also. How many times have you said "If only?" The distance between you and true happiness is only as great as your desire and willingness to work to change or remove an unpleasant situation.

Stress comes from many sources. It splinters and divides itself into many sharp pieces of reality. For example, think of all the reasons that a relationship can be severed. From what was once a good and happy union, much pain and misery can evolve.

Two souls become imbalanced, out of phase with each other. The resulting private, individual pain can become almost unbearable. Home, work, income, children, friends, relatives, all are caught up in the spiral of negativity and become disarranged.

Stress is like a disease. It spreads quickly to all areas of your life. The minute you recognize that you have been exposed to any kind of stress you should remove yourself emotionally from the situation as much as possible. Avoid overreacting and narrow down your thoughts and emotions to the actual reason for the stress. Don't immediately visualize how it is going to affect everyone or anything else in your life. Look at the cause objectively and keep your focus on it until you understand it thoroughly.

This approach requires inner strength and determination, but I can assure you that it works. Thoughts are living things: the minute you give in to fear and anticipation you impregnate all future possibilities with doubt and thus negate the solution.

Losing a job is not the end of the world; neither is severing a relationship. Discussing what happened and how it's going to affect your life is a deliberate effort on your part to manifest exactly what you dread. It's not easy to take command and be cool when every part of you wants to scream and cry. But it is much easier than suffering the consequences of falling into the stream of negative possibilities, for you will suffer a long time if you do.

## TIME DOES NOT HEAL

How often have you heard the clichéd phrase, "Time heals all wounds"? Well, I'm sorry to be the one to tell you that actually, time does not heal at all! Time has no healing effect whatsoever. YOU are the one who heals yourself. Over a period of time, the pain of a severance gradually subsides, but this is because you have gradually learned to accept reality. Unfortunately, for some this acceptance time can stretch out over a long period—years, in fact. As we endure the suffering, we see it reflected in other avenues of life. How then can traumatic circumstances be handled? Knowing that inevitably the pain will disappear, you have a choice of causing this to happen quickly or dragging the whole thing out. Prolonging the negativity is a form of emotional anesthetic. Give yourself plenty of time to adjust and rearrange your life.

## TAKING CHARGE

So where do you begin? How can you avoid extending unnecessary pain? Begin with you. Take charge of yourself. See exactly what is happening. Stop hindering your progress with various excuses. Move back emotionally and see the true situation. Imagine you are taking a mental photograph of the situation. The photograph will show everything exactly as it is. Every picture tells a story, so you don't need to write an article. It is what it is.

Pain is going to occur, but you can limit it by analyzing how much of your life was involved in the situation before its conclusion. It's obvious that you have invested a great part of yourself: all you feel now is a huge gap. You find it difficult to imagine anything else filling this space. This is the nucleus of your despair—the inability to immediately respond and program an alternate activity or relationship.

You have the power to accept the pain; you also have the power to release the pain. Maintaining the emotional bond is harmful, for by doing so you are energizing the original turmoil. A period of grief is acceptable and normal, even considered healthy. Beyond that it becomes a monster which you harbor inside. This monster is then free to attack you at any time. Stop feeding this monster and it will die quickly.

Part of the pain is always associated with who did what. That should tell you plenty. If you feel like a victim you are more inclined to hang on to your pain. If you inflict the pain you are more likely to release the memory. Ego becomes involved, also guilt. Often the words we use to sever a relationship are not really true. Breaking down the other person's belief system is a certain way to shatter what has existed between you.

I am not talking lightly of pain and relationships. I am trying to show you exactly how it works in conjunction with the mind. If the end result, regardless of any emotional outburst, does not include YOU, then there is absolutely no point in punishing yourself further.

So now you have reached the determining point of self-rescue. Of course it is impossible to see yourself instantly in a new job or in love with someone else. But it is possible to recognize a higher authority. It is possible to accept that you are experiencing an essential and painful episode of your karmic journey.

When something changes suddenly in your life, you have arrived at the Karmic Crossroads. How the change appears is not necessarily how it is. When you arrive at the various Karmic Crossroads, you are given a new direction. Reluctance to take another direction leaves you standing at the Crossroads and delays all the possible future events.

Be willing to open your heart and mind to alternative possibilities. Know that at your Karmic Crossroads you are being shown another path by which to express everything that you are. This path will take you into new and exciting possibilities once you release yourself from your previous thought patterns. You will experience new situations, people and places on your new path. Leave the past behind after your initial grief. Be strong and begin to look for your new life pattern. Emotional pain is a very real thing, but you are not meant to wallow in it. Stand up and look for the light. If it remains hidden, then ask for help. Not only will you receive light but also the strength to go on. There are many happy situations that you have yet to experience. Go forward and rid yourself of Karmic Stress. Move on—you are a special person. Respect your own karmic purpose and start to live NOW.

## MEDITATION 5: LETTING GO OF PAIN

This meditation is to help you disconnect from your emotional pain. First, it will show you how to let go of the energy used to maintain the negative influence. Then it will help you see the powerful forces that can assist you and will expose you to the wonderful possibilities available in your life.

1. Become acutely sensitive to your body. Feel the weight and heaviness deep inside. Focus all of your attention on your total weight: a combination of mental, spiritual and physical forces. Negativity in any form is a resisting force that the physical body absorbs. This causes you to feel weary and heavy on all levels.

2. Now visualize the reason for your pain. As you do this, allow the effect to come into the body. The heaviness appears to increase as your visualization becomes clearer and more vivid.

3. As you hold this mental picture, visualize a large GREEN SPHERE beneath your feet. Stretch your legs, ankles and toes till you feel your feet firmly on the GREEN sphere.

4. You now feel extremely heavy. The GREEN of the sphere beneath your feet is now cool, GREEN grass. It feels good; move your toes and feel firmly grounded.

5. Now focus your attention from your Inner Eye down through the center of your body. Down farther, through the feet and directly into the GREEN sphere. Inhale slowly a deep GREEN breath. Bring this breath to the Heart Chakra and hold for the count of THREE. Release and exhale PURE WHITE energy through the Heart Chakra.

6. Continue this method of breathing in a comfortable, relaxed manner. You are now bringing the original seed—the CAUSE —to the Heart. As you exhale pure WHITE, you are using universal energy—the light and power of God—to assist you in releasing your pain.

7. As the pure WHITE light is expelled through the Heart Chakra, it begins to build and take form before you. Watch this powerful vibratory force take shape.

8. As the form manifests, you feel the solace and comfort of a divine being. It is THE ANGEL GABRIEL. See and feel the power and love emanating from the Angel GABRIEL. As the glow of his heavenly power and protection surrounds you,

> ASK that your pain be healed.
> ASK for clarity of thought and action.
> ASK that you might retain the energy to eliminate the CAUSE.
> ASK for a new direction away from the pain.

9. The Angel GABRIEL now points to a cloud of BLUE energy. Walk into this energy and feel its penetrating, healing rays flood every cell of your body. Wait till the energy gradually fades away.

10. The Angel GABRIEL now points to a cloud of GOLDEN energy. Walk into this energy and feel the robust GOLDEN rays flood every cell of your body. Wait till the energy recedes.

11. As your vision now becomes clear, follow the Angel GABRIEL through a doorway and into a long corridor. There are many doors; look for the GOLDEN door. Walk in and see your immediate future WITHOUT pain. Take your time. When you are ready to leave, the Angel GABRIEL will come for you.

12. When you see the Angel GABRIEL again, give thanks for the absence of pain. Now go back through the GOLDEN door into the corridor. Walk back through the main door and see once again the cloud of BLUE energy. Stand in its center and once more feel its penetrating, healing rays enter every pore of your body.

13. Look high above your head and see the pure WHITE energy. Feel the firmness of the Root Chakra. Your feet are again standing on the GREEN sphere. Breathe in PURE WHITE through the Heart Chakra and release PURE WHITE by exhaling through the Heart Chakra.

14. Let your attention now focus on NEW seeds, NEW ways, NEW beginnings. You are full of inspiration and joy. Give thanks to the Angel GABRIEL and contemplate what you have seen for a few moments before recording your experience.

This peaceful and energizing meditation should be used for any situation that causes anguish or pain on any level.

## ARRIVING AT THE KARMIC CROSSROADS

Arriving at the Karmic Crossroads indicates major changes that require major choices. Sometimes you may arrive at these Crossroads unexpectedly. Other times you are given sufficient warnings, but ignore them. If a situation is not right, then it is certainly wrong! But subconsciously you find a way to adjust. This adjustment becomes the first of many. Finally, when your subconscious becomes aware that it can no longer adjust, the responsibility springs sharply into your conscious mind.

When your conscious mind receives this information, it no longer has the support and security of the hidden level of tolerance. It is immediately confronted by the responsibility. Any further action is monitored on this level; consequently, you become vulnerable to instant emotional pain.

Everyone experiences the terrific impact of arriving at the Karmic Crossroads. There are those who are mentally agile and can respond immediately by making major decisions. Maybe you are well trained in this area. Sadly, the average person is not always well equipped, and this results in the incapacity to deal with the situation objectively.

Every commitment, every relationship is susceptible to the power of karma. Knowing this and being alert to all that is happening in your life can prepare you for any possible change. Coping with change that intrudes on your level of security may induce trauma. Limiting yourself to the overindulgence of emotional instability will promote a more rapid change of events. This karmic chain reaction will then present you with a new set of life circumstances.

The following Meditation will help you prepare yourself to deal with your Karmic Crossroads.

## MEDITATION 6:  THE KARMIC CROSSROADS

1. As you physically and emotionally relax, see yourself standing at the Karmic Crossroads. Wait. . . .

2. Behind you is the path you have followed. Before you are two signposts. One leads to "Continuing Sorrow." The other leads to "New Opportunity." The first road looks comparatively easy. It is broad, open and full of familiar landmarks. The second road looks narrow and lonely. It appears steep and you can't see clearly because of the mist. Resist the temptation to walk on the Road of Continuing Sorrow. Prepare yourself for your journey on the Road to New Opportunity. Wait. . . .

3. Before you start your journey you must change your traveling clothes. Your clothing is soiled, but in your bag you have a RED gown of Individuality. Remove the soiled clothes and put on your RED gown. Wait. . . .

4. You are now ready and waiting for your spiritual companion. As you wait, focus in a determined manner on all the negative situations you are going to leave behind. At first your mind will bubble with this and that. Apply discipline and consider all the hurt you have experienced. Focus your mind on exactly what you must release. Wait. . . .

5. Your MASTER arrives, smiling reassuringly and asking what you intend to leave behind. Answer this question honestly. Wait. . . .

6. There are still things you find difficult to release. Speak openly to your Master about these things and ask for wisdom. Wait. . . .

7. Each of the situations you need to discard will present its own difficulties. So first you must determine the real problem, the true source of your stressful situation. Ask for help if you need it. Wait. . . .

8. Take this ONE problem with you as you walk down the Road of New Opportunity. Don't allow any other unrelated situation to interfere. In your RED gown of Individuality follow this road and meet all the resulting consequences of your decision. Face them all honestly and deal with each small possibility. Don't allow yourself to wander off this road. Be determined to apply the energy needed to rid yourself of any excuse. You are so tired of carrying this negative load. Wait. . . .

9. Concentrate and deal with your specific issues. Consider all the alternatives and allow new thoughts to enter. Wait. . . .

10. Over to your LEFT is the Moving River of Life. Splash your face and wash your feet. Feel your pain and past anxiety being washed away. See it all disappear in the fast-moving current. Stay here and permit peace to enter your soul. Regain your inner strength and make ready to continue your journey. See all your remaining doubts and fears leave you in the flow of rushing waters. Wait. . . .

11. Your Master now stands at your side. You feel radiant power surging through every part of your body. A new strength is rising within you. Wait. . . .

12. Once again focus on your life. Throw old ideas and concepts that are no longer feasible into the Moving River of Life. Do this now and feel the love of your Master supporting your decisions. Wait. . . .

13. You are now ready to walk alone and explore all the new possibilities. As you walk along the river bank, the Path of Inner Peace is to your RIGHT. Along this path are new and different life circumstances. You will see the changes that are now taking place. It is peaceful and you understand fully that you can make all these things happen. Look at your new life and the things you are going to do. Wait. . . .

14. Looking ahead, you see a WHITE marble temple with marble steps. The sun shines on the GOLDEN dome. It is a magnificent sight. Wait. . . .

15. As you approach the Temple, you see faint outlines of your lingering fears on the marble steps. These are the remaining shadows of negativity. You must climb these steps and face each shadow of fear. Confront each shadow with new determination. Your RED gown of Individuality is now glowing like CRIMSON fire. Your inner strength is building and as you climb the steps and walk into the shadows, boldly command them to LEAVE, saying: YOU ARE NOT A PART OF MY FUTURE JOY AND HAPPINESS. At your command the shadows will be replaced by glorious light. Remember that you are wearing the RED gown of Individuality. Your command once

again is: GO; YOU ARE NOT A PART OF MY FUTURE JOY AND HAPPINESS. As you reach the top of the marble steps, you feel jubilant. You have struggled and conquered the shadows of your fears. Enjoy your triumph, the happiness of regaining command. Wait. . . .

16. The Temple is full of WHITE light. Open the doors and enter. Go to the center of the Temple, under the GOLDEN Dome. Stand here and feel the WHITE light entering every part of your body. All your chakras are blazing with the force of the WHITE light. Wait. . . .

17. The WHITE light spirals around you. You are now rising UP, UP, UP into the GOLDEN Dome. As you enter the GOLD vibratory flow, you are totally renewed and replenished. Your prayers have been heard. You have been given strength. You are full of spiritual power. You are one with the Universal Spirit. Your heart opens with the light. Look, your gown is now pure WHITE. Your soul is ready to follow its own karmic path. You are FREE of your fears, finally free to be who you want to be. Wait. . . .

18. Now you are ready to start living. Feel yourself coming down to the Temple floor, slowly and majestically, in a GOLDEN spiral. As your feet touch the Temple floor, your heart is bubbling with your new spiritual freedom. Walk outside the Temple and see the steps before you all covered with ROSES. Your Master waits as you come down in joy. Wait. . . .

19. As you leave the last step, see before you a broad path. The sun is shining, birds are singing. Everything is absolutely beautiful in this new light. Your new life is before you. Say goodbye to your Master. Before you start the journey home on your new path, give thanks.

20. Say the following aloud:
    I AM SPIRITUALLY RENEWED AND FULL OF LIGHT.
    I HAVE MY LIFE TO LIVE AND I WILL LIVE IT NOW.
    I AM NO LONGER BOUND BY CHAINS OF FEAR.
    I AM THEE I AM. I AM THEE I AM. I AM THEE I AM.

21. Open your eyes and record your experience.

# CHAPTER 8

# REACHING BEYOND YOUR LIMITATIONS

We all have our daily work. It is vital that a portion of your daily energy be applied to the type of occupation you have. Fortunately, for some there is the added feeling of achievement and inner motivation. For others, the daily work schedule can be boring and oppressive. Whatever your daily routine is like, this chapter is especially for you. At school, office, home, on the road—wherever your daily task occurs —this period of working time is a necessity simply because it provides you with what you need to live the way you do.

Difficulties arise through boredom, insufficient remuneration, unsafe working conditions and lack of appreciation. Every day we allocate many slots in our minds, into which we file various portions of our responsibilities. Considering the amount of time we devote to our daily work routine, the remaining time is small. Many of us feel exhausted after completing our workday. Some have only enough energy left to watch TV; others have no energy left at all! Wives and children are neglected and life becomes gray and grim.

The need to work and earn a living is uppermost in almost everyone's mind. But after paying the mortgate or rent and all the other bills, you have to find space to be with yourself. You must provide yourself with "personal time." When my children were small, I called this "quiet time."

Not everyone has the best job, the best house or the best income. But all of us have the personal choice to allocate time for ourselves. Consider this time as space to think, really think. How long is it since you did this? So many people go from day to day, dealing with everything as it comes. Whatever life presents is dealt with at that moment.

At first it will seem strange to have quality time alone. You may not quite know what to do. You may find yourself turning on the radio or deciding to make a telephone call for no apparent reason other than to fill this space with normal activity. Allocate a piece of time entirely for yourself. Make a good habit of this and soon you will find it invaluable. Everyone needs a quiet period. Once you get used to it you will look forward to the solitude, and during this time you will begin to open your mind to new ideas and plans.

## KARMIC LIMITATIONS

Everyone has certain limitations in everyday existence. But over and above these limitations is your ability to explore, discover and enjoy everything that you are on all levels of consciousness. Sitting quietly in a chair, you can let your mind run free to expand and probe your karmic purpose, beyond the accepted limitations of your present life pattern.

Have you ever considered that the reason for your discontent could be karmic? If all the emphasis in your life is focused on the conscious level, perhaps the nagging discontent is what you are deliberately ignoring from other levels of consciousness. If you have a habit of pushing unwanted data into the subconscious level, then your Higher Consciousness is unable to penetrate and submit pertinent information. This information could totally change your present way of life! Think about it. All that you could possibly be and are is ready to be activated. Here is where free will comes into being: your personal choice to accept or reject limited conditions in your life.

Individuals who choose to live in the same house, in the same village and see the same people, year after year, would have difficulty in exposing themselves to the vast possibilities the world can offer. If you are tied to one level of consciousness, it could present the same obstacles. Your present life situation is perfect—*if you enjoy it*. But if you are continually struggling to expand and change your lifestyle, then you have the opportunity to explore your capacity for change.

## EXPLORING YOUR KARMIC DESTINY

The complexity of life is a result of karmic toil. Every human being, regardless of age, has their own karmic destiny. It is generally accepted that the knowledge in our karmic file is not available to us. I disagree with that. I have known many people who have taken the time and trouble to investigate their karmic purpose by using inner power and determination to retrieve karmic memory. I am not referring to hypnotism or regression, where you explore and retrieve past-life memory patterns and events. Every human being has an inherent ability to grow spiritually, to improve and progress on all levels of existence. Each of us can advance and feel the satisfaction of expressing every aspect of our individuality.

Regardless of the karmic lesson involved, we have the ability to open new facets of experience. Remember, this life is not a jail sentence! It is not totally confined to correcting past karmic errors. Contained within each lifetime is the chance to reveal other aspects of your soul potential. A depressed feeling of dissatisfaction may mean nothing more than that the Higher Self is reminding you of all the talent, creativity and opportunity remaining dormant through lack of effort on your part. The feeling of dissatisfaction arises through lack of understanding when you are severed from the intelligence of your Higher Self.

Karmic Meditation exercises usually do not bring instant results! It takes time to adjust and explore other levels of consciousness. Finding which exercise and procedure is best suited to your needs is the first step. Maybe just one will do, or several for alternate life situations. Begin with the basic seeds of inner desire. Allow yourself to bring these needs to the surface and to analyze your emotional balance.

Forming a group can help tremendously if you know others who are ready to be open and uncover hidden, embryonic gifts and skills. The preparation for meditation "sets the stage." Learn to breathe easily and follow the meditation steps. Don't feel rushed or hurried. Enjoy each phase of the process before going further. Allow ample time to thoroughly delve and expose yourself to the healing qualities of each vibratory plane. You will soon develop an expertise and your life will improve as you constantly strive to understand and perfect your journey in life.

# MEDITATION 7: REMOVING PERSONAL LIMITATIONS

1. Relax and recognize the restricting energies of self-imposed limitations. Make no effort to dwell upon any particular issue. Just continue to relax and allow the limitations to drift by.

2. As you do this, the limitations come closer and closer. You feel as though you are in the center of the restricting, negative force. YOU ARE.

3. Beginning at the Inner Eye, focus directly into the deep and beautiful color INDIGO.

4. As you inhale, feel yourself falling back into the comfort of the deep, soft INDIGO.

5. When you exhale you see far in front of you a tiny light. This light is where you entered the comfort and depth of the Inner Eye.

6. Each breath you inhale is comfortable and relaxing. You are moving back, back into the wisdom and warmth of the INDIGO.

7. You feel yourself moving away rapidly from the entrance to your chakras. Each outgoing breath pushes you farther back, yet you can still see the light of the entrance, now as a WHITE dot.

8. Relax as you proceed on your esoteric journey. Inhale a deep INDIGO breath; as you expel the breath, let your conscious mind acknowledge that you are extricating yourself from everything beyond the light of the chakra entrance.

9. Now feel yourself standing submerged in the vibratory force of INDIGO. Breathe in the INDIGO and breathe out all remaining negativity. Continue to do this in a very relaxed way until you feel totally absorbed in the spiritually energy of INDIGO. Take your time; there is no hurry, for we cannot go on until you are ready. . . .

10. Now the vibratory force of INDIGO is penetrating every cell. All your levels of consciousness are being bathed in the wisdom these vibrations give.

11. As the INDIGO enters every part of your being, you feel that you are expanding. It is a good, strong feeling.

12. Take a moment to absorb this spiritual strength. Enjoy the combination of wisdom and power; now focus your attention before you. See magnificent GOLD light move on a path before you.

13. You are now wearing a gown of INDIGO. Follow the GOLDEN light and know that each step you take is exhilarating on all spiritual levels.

14. Before you is a large house;the GOLDEN light enters the house. Wait awhile and listen. You hear and recognize voices. You want to enter the house.

15. The front door opens, and surrounded by the magnificent GOLDEN light, you see YOURSELF in perfect health, smiling and inviting you to enter. This is your HIGHER SELF. YOU at your very best. YOU with all knowledge. You feel very happy as you see your Higher Self dressed in radiant GOLD, looking wise and confident.

16. Your robe of INDIGO feels warm and comfortable. You enter the house. Your Higher Self invites you to wander at will and explore every room. Your Higher Self smiles encouragingly as you go to the first door.

17. This is the Room of Creativity. Open the door and enter. Absorb every detail and converse freely with anyone who is there. No other aspect of your life will be seen or discussed other than your creativity. Allow time to experience this fully. . . .

18. It is now time to visit your Rooms of Relationships. As you walk through your house, you will see the Relationship Doors. Each will have a name. Choose one to enter. If someone is there, converse freely. If you are directed to another room, you may go and find the room. You will see directly into the relationships presented, from this life or a past life. Relax and explore them. Allow time to experience this fully. . . .

19. You are now ready to enter the Door of Your Future Potential. You may see faces you have never seen before. Be alert, ask

any questions and observe what is shown to you. Allow time to experience this fully. . . .

20. Your Higher Self is now waiting to take you back. You now leave the House of your Subconscious. Look back at the house and know that both blockages and opportunities can exist in this place. This is your house. You may visit it anytime. Know that you can learn, relax and enjoy. Know also that you may be confronted with new challenges and opportunities. The next time you visit you can go to your own personal room, furnished according to your own true desire. Here you will be able to rest and recoup your energy. You also have the power to reflect on the past and improve it. This is your house, the House of the Subconscious.

21. As you prepare to go, see your Higher Self radiant with the power of self-confidence. Embrace and absorb your Higher Self into you. Feel the GOLDEN rays penetrate your robe of INDIGO. Breathe in the GOLDEN energy and let it flow into every part of your physical body.

22. Now walk forward through the wisdom of INDIGO. Your GOLDEN robe is scintillating with new and exciting energies. When you see the WHITE light before you, step forward and inhale THREE deep, comfortable breaths. Be still for a while; then be sure to record your experience for future reference.

# CHAPTER 9

# DECISIONS, DECISIONS

When you reach the point of having to make a decision but cannot do it, maybe this is not the time! Perhaps you'll make the right decision another day, a week later—or five minutes later. Once you release yourself from the pressure of *having* to make the decision, you automatically allow more thinking and feeling space.

I'm not trying to oversimplify the process of decision-making, nor downplay the seriousness of it. I know that deadlines, important issues and hurt feelings can be involved. Also, the more important the decision is, the more vital it is that you make the right one.

Some people can handle decision-making very easily. Others are always hesitant, thinking of alternatives. Actually, your personality has nothing to do with making a decision. It may color the decision but it has nothing to do with making it.

Gentle people can make exceptionally hard decisions. Strong, outgoing people can make weak decisions. The secret of making a good decision is to allow a measure of flexibility for all concerned.

Shouting at the world and declaring rigid and unbreakable edicts immediately prevents you from making further decisions. I have seen people live in pain for many years simply because an original decision was made and "cast in concrete." Although there was a later desire to change, pride and obstinacy prevented an old issue from healing.

Emergency decisions are aided by the Higher Self. If you have been in this type of situation, you probably wondered where your strength to deal with the problem came from. This is not the decision-making I am referring to. I'm talking about everyday or once-in-a-while decision-making, which is vitally important to personal progress and development.

# THE FEAR OF MAKING DECISIONS

There are those who avoid decisions and very seldom make them. This shows in their character and relationships. There are others who are far too hasty and quick to decide an issue; they are constantly battling life.

Then we have the "accident cases"—the victims. They find themselves unable to oppose a decision for fear of damaging their relationship with a partner, parent or friend. As a child, decisions are made for us. As we grow and mature, we learn how to make our own decisions or allow others to do it for us. If we accept a decision without approving of it because of insecurity or fear, the results can be devastating.

Avoiding decision-making because you fear what you say will hurt someone is wrong. The focus here should be on the presentation of the decision. You can see that if the decision you are going to make is not going to be appreciated, then how you state it may not be appreciated either. It is only later that the method of decision-making will be considered—the way you said it, your reason for doing it. This background will be a part of the healing process after the decision has been delivered. So try to present a decision as gently and tactfully as possible.

The people who suffer are the ones who have a decision to make but are afraid. They don't want to hurt the other person involved, but they are experiencing pain because they need to make the decision and can't.

A decision is the result of a desired change. Whether it is a need to leave your job, get married, sever a relationship or move to a new apartment, it is you trying to satisfy YOU. Your reluctance to make this decision comes from your feeling that your decision may not be acceptable to the party or parties concerned.

Before making any decision, you should consider all aspects carefully. If you still feel the need to make the decision, then you must make it in the best way possible. Decision-making effects the emotional level. Once a decision is made, it triggers the need for others to make decisions. The energy transmitted touches the emotional level of others, but not necessarily in the same way as yours!

Whenever there is a decision to be made and it is avoided, the free flow of natural energies becomes stagnant and inoperative. In these unnatural circumstances relationships become strained and threatened.

Every day we all have many decisions to make. They are made with little or no trauma because they do not penetrate the emotional level. For example, your job may involve constant decision-making for eight hours a day. You make these decisions with little or no difficulty. Yet you become reticent and weak when a relatively insignificant decision comes up that has an emotional attachment. There is a reluctance to let go of the familiar. Guilt feelings arise, creating fears that sometimes appear insurmountable.

The dread of decision-making can be eliminated if the decision you make comes from a balanced level. Regardless of the consequences, you *will* survive! Fear of the unknown can reduce a person to the emotional level of a child. If you hesitate and allow yourself to live according to the decisions of others, you will become submissive and dull.

Now we arrive at the unsophisticated source of this problem. Since time began, man has relied entirely on his instinctive ability to make decisions. In primitive times, survival was uppermost in his mind. Civilization and modern existence in many ways has dulled the ancient tool of man's survival—the natural and uncluttered skill of decision-making.

It is the lack of decision-making that makes firm decisions necessary. Attending to our basic needs and building good, loving relationships are vital to our nature. The desire to avoid these responsibilities for the sake of keeping a temporary peace simply does not work. When you avoid making a decision regarding your career, for example, the "domino" effect causes your loved ones to suffer without understanding why. The inability to make minor decisions inevitably creates the need for a major one.

When all that you are reflects in all that you do, you are well on your way to a happy and balanced life. Incidentally, dealing with these situations on a daily basis will eliminate the need to cope with heartbreaking decisions later. Remember what I said earlier? You can learn to cultivate this capacity and gather strength for making emergency decisions. You can also plan major decisions well ahead of time if you are hindered by insignificant minor decisions that have been ignored and have become long overdue.

## COURAGE AND PERSONAL POWER

Courage is imbedded in the soul of every man and woman. Our focus in the following meditation is to exercise our PERSONAL

POWER. The spiritual quality of Courage must first be energized with Personal Power. That is, a conscious effort must be undertaken to allow the quality of Courage to be manifested.

Courage is an inherent quality of the soul. Fine causes, true beliefs and the absence of fear open the depths, and Courage rises to inflame your intent. This happens when you take full control of your thoughts, words and actions. Being totally convinced of your inner motivations requires the application of Personal Power. These ingredients have combined in the elixir of all noble souls throughout time.

To show Courage is to touch upon your own soul. The man earning a little wage but supporting a wife and family struggles with his existence, yet he accepts the responsibility and becomes adept in showing his Courage. Bluster and idle threats are things of the ego, not to be confused with true Courage.

Making major decisions often requires Courage. To become courageous you must first take personal control to obtain the POWER which will flood all levels of your consciousness and accurately direct you to your correct choice.

Begin by contemplating your need for Courage. Consider the situations in which you must apply the quality of Courage. It doesn't take Courage to make easy decisions. Take a good, long look at the barriers that are there simply because you did not have the Courage to demolish them at the right time.

Once this realization enters your conscious level and you accept your deep need for Courage, you will be ready to generate your Personal Power. As your power expands, Courage will automatically flow in the identical vibratory stream. From that point on you can free yourself from all your restrictive barriers. Loved ones will come closer and new souls will know you by your personal LIGHT.

## MEDITATION 8: DISCOVERING THE SOURCE

1. Relax and wrap yourself gently in sunny YELLOW vibrations. Do this until you feel warm and comfortable. From head to toe spin the warm YELLOW vibrations protectively around your body.

2. As you continue to do this, become aware that all tension is leaving you.

3. Feeling light and relaxed, now focus your attention on your feet.

4. Move your toes and ankles easily without effort. Feel like a child wading in water as you immerse your feet in the warm, sunny, YELLOW light.

5. Gradually, without haste or tension, allow this warm, sunny YELLOW to rise up to your lower legs and knees. Take your time and flex your leg muscles and knees, allowing the YEL-LOW to saturate every area.

6. Again feel like a little one standing in a warm pool. The sun is overhead and the water is reflecting the radiance of its YEL-LOW energy.

7. Now with your hands splash the warm YELLOW water over your thighs and lower abdomen. Now sit in the GOLDEN pool. Enjoy the relaxing, soothing YELLOW vibrations.

8. Feel the GOLDEN pool now rise up and over your breast. Notice how your shoulders totally relax as the YELLOW vibrations now gently soothe your neck . . . up and over your chin . . . over your lips and eyes and up to your Inner Eye.

9. Now with your inner focus, visualize a flash of WHITE light as the soothing YELLOW-GOLD vibrations pass over this chakra.

10. Your head now tilts slightly forward as the GOLDEN radiance circulates through the conscious, subconscious and Higher Conscious levels. It is a wonderful, powerful feeling. You are being completely penetrated by the vibratory power of GOLD. Inside your body you feel it moving and energizing every vital organ.

11. Concentrate on this spiritual process. Follow the energy as it caresses every cell of your body. You are becoming renewed and refreshed and filled with energy.

12. Enjoy this spiritual experience. To your LEFT you see a GOL-DEN CHALICE materializing out of the swirling gold vibrations. It is being handed to you. Take it and feel the beauty of

this Golden Chalice. Look at it closely, so you will recognize it another time.

13. You now feel a deep desire to drink the spiritual elixir contained in the Chalice. You must empty the Chalice completely. Each sip you take will increase your strength on all levels. Drink slowly and enjoy this experience fully.

14. When you finish drinking, the Chalice will fill up with deep INDIGO. You must now look and concentrate through your Inner Eye. Push gently as the strength of the GOLD aids your spiritual effort.

15. See yourself walk out of the GOLDEN pool and feel a warm INDIGO robe placed around you. As you look toward the trees ahead, you will see your MASTER. You greet each other warmly.

16. Sit down by the trees and acknowledge the Personal Power that has been given to you. Now ask that you be given COURAGE. Your MASTER will now talk with you as you reveal your cause, your need for Courage.

17. He may show you past-life or future-life scenes. You are strong and full of Personal Power. Be confident and assured. Listen to the wisdom of your Master. Take time for this procedure. . . .

18. When you are ready to return, look toward the golden pool. Lie down, wrapped in your INDIGO robe. Contemplate the wisdom you have received and give thanks.

19. As you allow yourself to come fully back to your conscious level, be aware of the increased vibratory force. See BLUE and WHITE flashes around your body, like sparks from steel. Allow this energy to merge into your aura and into the center of your body.

20. The pulsating energy from your Umbilical Chakra is now radiating a powerful YELLOW force. You are now the center of the SUN. Feel the rays extending from you.

21. You are blessed—you now have the gift of COURAGE. Allow the vibratory force to subside and relax for a while. Then open your eyes and record your experience.

CHAPTER 10

# PRAYER AND THE ETHERIC BODY

Meditation is the highest form of prayer. When a person consciously reaches for spiritual levels, this is prayer, and it can relieve the body of various forms of stress. Focusing on higher levels allows the Etheric Body to rejuvenate the physical body. (We'll discuss the Etheric Body later in this chapter.)

The physical body has several control centers. Without the input of spirituality the body is controlled mainly through the conscious, physical level. When stress is present, it is directly reflected in the physical body. The cause of stress is registered physically but is not necessarily recognized on the conscious level. It could be the result of past stress surfacing and demanding spiritual attention.

You could say that "Original Karma" is the first source of all stress, but covered over by layers of time and neglect, it is seldom understood. Under normal conditions the Etheric Body continually replenishes the physical body. Problems arise when your focus is directed solely upon material matters in your everyday life. You may tend to ignore the physical body when you're busy, and when pain occurs you resort to medicine. In other words, you take your physical health for granted until you experience discomfort. Then you tend to treat the result instead of searching for the cause.

The ancient procedures are still effective. Some of the old methods are still used and have been absorbed into contemporary healing methods. You can go beyond this complexity directly to the simple, basic truths. The first step is to allow your mind to go beyond your physical problem. Once you accomplish this you are well on your way to the source of your stress.

Your focus for self-healing is not on the RESULT but the CAUSE. When you understand this, you can access the universal energies, which are pure and untouched. Availing yourself of this energy source can eliminate all negative consequences.

PHYSICAL DISEASE OCCURS SIMPY BECAUSE THE BODY IS ILL AT EASE; THAT IS, IT IS "DIS-EASED."

Any departure from complete health signifies that the physical body is not truly in balance. The source of this imbalance is located OUT-SIDE the physical body and BEYOND normal everyday consciousness.

If recognizing the true source of an ailment is overshadowed by fear and conscious reasoning, fortunately we have modern-day medicine and surgical procedures available. I am not suggesting that a doctor should not be called upon for advice and treatment. Obviously, it would be unwise for a sick person to ignore medical attention. But if the ancient spiritual procedures were absorbed and used as a normal way of life, it would be unlikely that your health would deteriorate as rapidly as is generally expected. Growing old, for example, would not be as traumatic. Leaving this life could be a peaceful process, knowing that you will once again be rebirthed.

Prayer and mediation are the ancient procedures that can help us recognize the real source of our illnesses and stress, so that we can deal with them effectively.

## THREE FORMS OF PRAYER

Basically, there are three forms of prayer:

### 1. The Asking Prayer

This is the type of prayer through which you ask or implore the Powers That Be to make something happen in your life. Sometimes there is an attempt to bargain: If you grant me this, I will do that in return.

## 2. The Prayer of Intercession

In this type of prayer you ask some holy entity to intercede for you in some matter, to "put in a good word" on your behalf. A person may feel unworthy to approach God directly on a personal basis, so they ask a saint, angel or Christ to speak on their behalf.

## 3. The Meditation Prayer

Not everyone associates the act of prayer with meditation. It is generally assumed that meditation is a spiritual act that is totally "Eastern" and that not everyone can do it, especially in the West. This is not so; anyone can learn to meditate. Meditation is the highest form of prayer, because nothing is asked for. The soul simply opens itself to whatever wisdom it can absorb to elevate itself to a higher level of spirituality.

# THE SIMPLICITY OF MEDITATION

Prior to meditating, the conscious level chooses to relax and allow the soul to find its spiritual source. Regardless of the reason for meditating, your Inner self has already decided to meet its needs on a spiritual level unblemished by its own reasoning power. It is aware of your need, yet allows the God Force to enlighten or manifest without judgment or expectation.

It is not a matter of whether your prayer is answered or not. A measure of spiritual solace is obtained from the simple experience of meditating itself. You always receive a result from meditative practice, even though your conscious mind may not recognize it.

Sometimes things are so simple and obvious, we never see them! The source of healing is also simple, but it requires you to take a good look at basic esoteric principles before you can apply them effectively. To do this you must first consider the Etheric Body. Once you understand exactly what it is, you will be ale to avail yourself of hitherto unknown spiritual energies.

# THE ETHERIC BODY

What is the Etheric Body and where is it? It is the womb or matrix which to some degree controls the balance and stability of the physical body.

The Etheric body continually strives to maintain the equilibrium of the Astral and Mental Bodies—the Outer Bodies—in relation to the physical body. The Etheric Body is located between the Outer Bodies and the physical body. Acting as a point of stabilization, it ensures that the physical body reflects a true image of the inherent soul qualities. The Etheric Body exists outside the physical body and is affected by both the Astral and Mental bodies.

To fully grasp this concept, you must understand that the Etheric Body receives its input of spirituality from the Outer Bodies. In turn it endeavors to extend these qualities to the physical body. Perfect health is just one of these possibilities. The Etheric Body is identical to the physical body and represents all that can be considered physically healthy. Its deterioration occurs when the conscious mind willingly or unwillingly allows a negative flow of energy to inundate the physical structure.

Visualize an exact reproduction of your physical body but perfect in every way, with access to your higher levels of consciousness. This is your Etheric Body. Our ancient fathers had ready access to it. It has been taught and written about often, sometimes in complicated philosophical treatises. My intention is to extract the vital essence of those early works and convey the knowledge in a straightforward, practical manner.

This knowledge is applicable to your situation, therefore it does not challenge your intellect. It has only to be discovered and used correctly and you will find yourself looking and feeling years younger! Let me repeat the KEY:

VISUALIZE AN EXACT REPRODUCTION OF YOUR PHYSICAL BODY, PERFECT IN EVERY WAY, WITH ACCESS TO YOUR HIGHER LEVELS OF CONSCIOUSNESS.

The Etheric Body is formulated first. The physical body is a reflection of the Etheric Body. A perfect physical body is designed to mature and retain its perfection. I am not referring to the natural aging process, but the ability to maintain good physical health.

As the physical body matures, the Etheric Body reaches a spiritual level of maturity and maintains that peak throughout life. It is through this basic knowledge that one can see clairvoyantly clear evidence of the Etheric Body.

We've all heard of soldiers who have lost limbs during a war. It is a well-known fact that long after outward physical healing has taken place the soldier can still experience excrutiating pain in the missing limb. The reason for this is that the Etheric Body has *not* lost a limb! The influence of the Etheric Body gives the soldier a feeling that the limb still exists. What we must understand is that the limb *does* exist in the Etheric Body. As the limb was severed quickly, the Etheric Body has to adjust, and until it does it will create the sensation of physical pain. Eventually the soldier's pain will ease, but in many cases, long after the pain has gone, the soldier will still feel the missing limb as though it were a part of his body.

This knowledge helped the ancient fathers understand the karmic implications of deformity at birth. As they were able to view the body clairvoyantly, they could see whether the infant's Etheric Body was also deformed. If so, they knew that the soul had elected to enter life with a specific purpose which involved deficiencies in the physical body. These souls were treated with great respect, for according to the ancient wisdom, they had elected to devote their lives to correcting their karmic destiny.

## THE AURA

The aura is invisible to the human eye. It is an essence that emanates not only from human beings and animals but also from minerals and plants. It has been said that the halos depicted around the heads of Jesus Christ and the saints are in fact examples of pure auras. Consider the aura as a reflection between the physical and Etheric Bodies. If all is well and in balance, this can be seen through the rays of the aura. So too can illness be detected here. The aura is similar to a thermometer in that it registers the type of activity being experienced. As the emotional level is also reflected in the aura, you can see why the aura is a changing phenomenon.

Have you ever watched the setting sun? The changing shapes and colors occur so rapidly. I have stood on the beach and watched the magnificent orange of the burning sun quickly turn into gorgeous pinks and purples. Like a child, I have felt amazed by how quickly it all disappears and the sky becomes dark. Auras can do exactly the same!

## ETHERIC MEDITATION

The Etheric Body contains your source of health and well-being. It provides that last bit of energy you didn't think you had. The Etheric Body has often prevented you from many serious accidents. The "physical knowing" is the unknown communication between you and your Etheric Body. Isn't it time you introduced yourself?

Everything you are and everything you can be is contained within the Etheric Body. If you choose to ignore its existence, you deprive yourself of all its benefits. Life becomes a mysterious uphill challenge, when in fact it is possible to tune into the karmic structure of who you are. You can begin to eliminate Karmic Stress immediately when you recognize the untouched power that can be yours.

The fusion of etheric energies helps to expel lingering negative tendencies in the physical body. Once this is accomplished, the continuance of etheric meditation will reinforce all your weak areas. Karmic Stress can be eliminated with time and practice through attention to the Etheric Body.

Your focus begins *not* in the Etheric Body but in the physical body. By allowing our conscious mind to scan the physical body deeply, you create an esoteric vibration that is capable of rebuilding any weak or damaged area. This etheric energy will first concentrate on the physical level and then merge into the higher levels of consciousness.

At the point in your development when the other levels of consciousness merge, you will be touching upon your karmic purpose, receiving knowledge and wisdom that will open new vistas of life. All meditation exercises should be practiced with patience and regularity. It is good to focus on different levels for different purposes. Using only one method of meditation can create an unbalanced activity in any one chakra. For this reason you should try all the various meditation exercises and select at least three to use over a period of time.

Study the purpose of each meditation. See which are best suited to your physical, mental and spiritual goals. Make a disciplined plan to practice your meditations. Frequent and regular time periods will produce substantial results.

## MEDITATION 9: THE ETHERIC FOCUS

1. Relax completely. Let your consciousness focus directly on your physical body. If your mind starts to wander, gently bring your thoughts back to your body.

2. During this part of the meditation your conscious level is in control. Now begin to think of your toes. Concentrate on your toes. You do not need any color influence here. Just concentrate on your toes and move them gently.

3. Now move your attention into your feet. Let your concentration build for a moment and then move your feet gently.

4. Now bring the focus to your ankles. Hold for a moment and rotate your ankles gently to the left. Now gently to the right.

5. Your attention now reaches the calves of your legs. Flex the calf muscles in a very relaxed way. Hold this focus for a count of THREE.

6. Now focus on your knees. Hold for a moment, then consciously activate the energy in your knees.

7. As you go up to the thighs, relax and focus on every part of your thighs. Take your time; when ready, hold your focus for a count of three. Feel the focus spreading throughout the thigh area.

8. The focus now is on your lower abdomen. Don't let it go beyond this area. Feel your attention flood the lower abdomen until you have the complete area in your focus. Hold for a count of three.

9. Raise your focus now to the umbilical area. It feels good—you need to take your time. Scan the entire umbilical area and then hold.

10. Bring your attention to your midriff. Be aware that you are now concentrating on the emotional level. Keep your concen-

tration focused and flood the whole emotional belt with your complete attention. Hold for a count of three.

11. Keeping relaxed and in command, now slowly bring your attention up to the chest and heart area. Let your mind absorb the complete area. Do not feel hurried; relax and explore your heart and lungs. Hold your attention for a count of three.

12. The focus is now on your shoulder. Hold it there for just a moment. Now let your attention slip down both arms very slowly and easily. Feel your focus as it travels down through your arm muscles and into the elbow joints. Now let it drop into the lower arms and wrists. As your attention is now on the wrists, move them gently and allow the focus to go into the palms of your hands. At this point hold your concentration for a count of three. Now allow the focus to travel into your fingers and thumbs.

13. As you reach the tips of your fingers, let the strength of your concentration now reverse the flow and bring your focus back up to the shoulders. Now move up to the throat area. As your attention reaches here, let it move around in the neck and into the back of your throat. Hold this for a count of three.

14. From the back of your throat, lift your attention to all parts of your head. With your focus remaining at the back of the throat, once again hold for a count of three.

15. From the center back of the throat, direct your attention out to both ears. Feel that you are exploring all of these areas.

16. Leaving the ears, bring your focus into the mouth. Let the tongue, palate and teeth become aware of your focus. Hold this focus for a count of three.

17. Feel your attention now rising up, up, up into the top of your head. Let your focus explore and settle in every cell. Take your time; probe with your focus and slowly bring your attention to the top center of your head. Hold again for a count of three.

18. Allow your attention to rise up and OUT of the top center of your head. As you accomplish this, let your focus now FALL before you. Wait for it to fall and see it build into a WHITE light.

19. Let the WHITE light circle around you. See it climb up and over your head. Now direct it back beneath your feet. Hold your attention here for a count of FOUR.

20. Now visualize the WHITE light once again building before you. As it reaches the Umbilical Chakra, INHALE a deep YELLOW breath and bring it directly into the center of your body.

21. As the energy disperses throughout the body, feel the rays of the Umbilical Chakra extend in brilliant GOLDEN YELLOW. Hold this in a relaxed manner for the count of TEN.

22. Now feel all the energies completely subside. Every part of your body is now alert and full of new energy. INHALE one deep breath of GREEN; as you EXHALE, relax completely and give thanks. . . .

This meditation will transmit healthy vibrations throughout your physical body. Your Etheric Body cannot be depleted, as it exists in a continuous state of vibratory power. As you deliberately extract and transfer its energies, they are continually renewing themselves from the higher levels.

Many esoteric scholars are unaware of the many benefits of this meditation procedure. The mere act of conscious focus extracts all the health-giving qualities that the physical body requires. Focus ALONE can do this. But it must be monitored and done in the above sequence.

Although initially it may appear difficult to focus over this time period, eventually you will develop the meditative skill. Unless you are in control consciously there will be no obvious benefits, so you should not do the Etheric Meditation if you are tired.

As you direct your conscious focus in this meditation, the Etheric Body expands. The mere act of disciplined focus produces an input of healthy vibrations from the Etheric Body. Constant practice of this meditation will supply the body with strong health-giving energies. As the physical body absorbs these energies, you will benefit greatly from improved physical and mental health.

CHAPTER 11

# THE CHAKRAS

The Sanskrit word "chakra" means "wheel." The chakras are spiritual energy centers in the body; their positions are often related to locations in the physical body, but in fact the chakras are located in the Etheric Body. To better describe their placement and functions, we locate them in the physical body.

There are seven major chakras, numbered one through seven, beginning with the lowest vibrational frequency and proceeding upward to the highest. There are also many minor chakras, which are stimulated by the activity of the seven major chakras, but we will focus our study on the major centers. Each chakra has several qualities by which it is identified. These include

COLOR
SANSKRIT NAME
ASSOCIATED GLAND(S)
LIFE AREA

To take an example, the CROWN Chakra (Number 7) is located at the exact top center of the head. It is actually on the surface of the Etheric head. A clairvoyant would see this chakra as a moving, spinning vortex of color, constantly rotating as it manifests divine energy directly into the physical body.

As a person develops spiritually, the chakras reflect this development in the same way as an athlete's muscles develop. Just as an athlete is able to make his body do more than the average man, so does a spiritually developed person gain access to other areas of expression that are considered psychic.

Chakras are spiritual areas in the Etheric Body which collect, hold and distribute a continuous flow of PRANIC or spiritual energy. Our esoteric approach and meditation procedures will induce the appropriate vibratory flow, which will admit a substantial input of Prana to initiate the level or balance required.

Releasing stress can be enhanced by using the chakras. A vigorous chakra emitting vital life energies is the result of spiritual exercise and focus. Life-giving forces are continually being transmitted from the Etheric Body to the physical body. When chakras are opened, the spiritual energy released exhilarates and arouses the spiritual, mental and physical levels.

The initial impact of this energy provides the impetus needed to correct your spiritual balance. Once this level is achieved, a feeling of well-being is established which is a prerequisite to a healthy, happy existence.

As our study in this book is not directly focused on the chakras, let it suffice to say that a complete study of these spiritual centers can be both enlightening and rewarding. It is a deep and profound study for the esoteric student. Ancient teachings regarding the chakras contain valuable philosophy that the present-day spiritual scholar will find necessary to a serious search for knowledge.

In further study you will find that various authors claim different names and positions for the chakras. This does not matter. In Oriental mysticism, they are referred to as the organs of the Astral Body and also as lotus flowers. When the chakras develop, the "petals of the lotus" open.

## THE COLORS OF THE CHAKRAS

As each chakra radiates with Pranic energy, its vibratory force emits variations of color. For example, the CROWN Chakra is an absolute wonder of indescribable beauty as many tones and shades of color pulsate with the input of Prana.

There is an outer and an inner activity of color change with the Crown Chakra. It is considered to be the most magnificent of all. When man has discovered his spiritual purpose and path, it is said that the Crown Chakra elevates above the head in a halo of brilliant divine light, appearing as a sort of heavenly crown.

Exposure to the seven colors does affect the rhythm of the chakra system as a whole. Whenever you are confronted with a huge array of color, you are definitely affected in some way! In my research I have found that although people seem to react strongly to a multicolored source, what happens, in fact, is that the reaction is triggered by the brilliance or energy of one or more individual hues. These can be determined by the process of elimination.

For example, babies at the height of their physical energy react well to all seven colors. As they become tired, they reject the multicolors and prefer their natural O Level colors found in their given name at birth (see: *Connolly Book of Numbers, Vol. I*). As a baby becomes physically tired, he is not able to assimilate all the colors; only those that are comfortable, as determined by his O Level.

As the child develops, he begins to have favorite colors and indicates his preference. However, it is not unusual for a child to reject a color from his O Level. This is the result of the type of energy that each specific color represents. If the child is encountering mental, physical or spiritual difficulties or challenges in the area of activity that the color represents on his O Level, this would account for his rejection of a particular color or colors.

The adult often avoids certain colors for the same reason as a child. Esoteric study or counseling can correct this reaction to color and bring about a vast improvement in attitude, enthusiasm and energy.

When viewed clairvoyantly, the seven colors of the seven major chakras are seen to vary in shade and intensity. These variations are determined by the body's spiritual balance. Lighter and darker shades monitor the emotional level, for example. Meditation practice helps considerably to modify and stabilize chakra colors.

# THE QUALITIES OF THE CHAKRAS

| Number | English Name | Sanskrit Name | Location | Gland(s) | Life Area | Color |
|---|---|---|---|---|---|---|
| 1 | Root | Muladhara | Base of spine | Ovaries/ Testes | Foundations of life | RED |
| 2 | Sacral | Swadhisthana | Sacral region, below the navel | Spleen | Life force, sexuality, | ORANGE |
| 3 | Umbilical | Manipura | Solar plexus | Adrenals | Personal power courage, determination | YELLOW |
| 4 | Heart | Anahata | Over the heart | Thymus | Peace, harmony, balance | GREEN |
| 5 | Throat | Vishuddha | Front of throat | Thyroid | Creativity, karmic potential | SKY BLUE |
| 6 | Inner Eye | Ajna | Forehead, between the eyebrows | Pituitary | Spiritual wisdom and development | INDIGO |
| 7 | Crown | Sahasrara | Center top of the head | Pineal | Universal concept | VIOLET |

# THE ROOT CHAKRA

Although the ROOT Chakra is located in the reproductive area, it is actually energized below the feet. To activate the Root Chakra, the focus begins in a sphere visualized directly under the feet. The energy is then consciously raised from the sphere, up through the feet and legs to the base of the spine. At this time, with the correct method and procedure, the Root Chakra will begin to energize.

The initial color focus to release the required energy from the sphere is GREEN. As the vibratory flow of GREEN rises to the Root Chakra, it becomes RED. It increases in power and intensity as the motivating force of GREEN merges completely into the chakra and becomes entirely RED.

The momentum of the chakra force will again change its color, especially in highly developed spiritual activity. The Life Area which this Chakra influences is the Foundations of man. At the critical point of contact the chakra divides into four sections—an X-shaped cross within a circle. This cross fluctuates from RED to ORANGE, giving it a fiery appearance.

FOR THE PURPOSE OF MEDITATION WE USE THE COLOR THAT ACTIVATES THE CHAKRA INITIALLY. COLOR THAT DE-VELOPS BEYOND THE PRIMARY INDICATES THE SPIRITUAL LEVEL ATTAINED.

## THE SACRAL CHAKRA

The SACRAL Chakra is considered to be partially developed. The complexity of conscience can maintain balance when the pure WHITE Light of Divinity is focused on this chakra.

All chakras can be stimulated in this way. When you add pure WHITE light to the chakra, it responds in its own color sequence. This form of meditation requires time and concentration and also the ability to keep spiritually focused until the transformation takes place and is felt on all levels—mental, spiritual and physical.

The warm glow of fiery ORANGE can be directed as a powerful force in all aspects of life. Think of the chakras and their corresponding colors as keys to higher learning and development. This type of medi-tation excludes everything but the color exercise involved. You must allow sufficient time to reach the peak of energizing the specific chakras. Their healing qualities are invaluable. Each separate chakra should be meditated upon in sequence, one through seven.

## THE UMBILICAL CHAKRA

This vulnerable chakra area immediately responds to your deepest emotions, provide self-mastery and assisting you to direct your life according to your true inner desire. When out of balance over a period of time, the UMBILICAL Chakra's motion is affected and the body responds physically.

This chakra is the center of your being. You should visualize this area as your SUN Center. Clear, beautiful YELLOW vibrations solid-ify into a warm and protective sphere. A good attitude and good rela-tionships create a force that causes rays to extend out from the chakra into your aura. Imagine, if you will, a sun in the center of your body.

Happiness and personal confidence allow the power of this sun to nourish your aura.

Meditation which involves directing pure WHITE light into the Umbilical Chakra makes an excellent start to a special day. Wearing a chakra color can be complementary to the purpose of your meditation. My personal symbol for this important chakra is the SUN.


## THE HEART CHAKRA

This chakra brings feelings of peace regardless of interference and outside opinions. Being the FOURTH chakra, it is the interchange of the lower three and upper three chakras. The HEART Chakra can be considered the point of acceptance on many levels.

The Heart Chakra needs substance to radiate its own unique level of spirituality. Bringing the GREEN light from the sphere below the feet into the second and third chakras magnifies the vibratory power as it reaches the Heart Chakra. There the GREEN from the Foundation merges in exquisite tones with the GREEN that constantly flows from the Heart Chakra.

This special spiritual exercise allows the seeds planted in your Foundation to be recognized fully. The GREEN energy flows through the Sacral Chakra, combining with the ORANGE, which rapidly ascends to the Umbilical Chakra, stirring the YELLOW energies into a burning sun. As this power merges, the rays shoot out into your aura. This personal power is then lifted up to the Heart Chakra. As a mother embraces her child, so does the Heart absorb the fresh GREEN vibrations, which are inundated with SEEDS. As GREEN meets GREEN, the vibratory flow penetrates all levels of consciousness.

The Heart Chakra is receptive and compassionate. Using it as an incoming center for healing can create amazing results. The power of the Heart Chakra is incredible. As the physical body relies on the heart to pump blood throughtout the body, so does the chakra system channel vital energies to the lower three and upper three chakras.

# THE THROAT CHAKRA

A strong tie exists between the THROAT Chakra and the INNER EYE Chakra. It is seldom acknowledged or used, yet the connection between the two carries a flow of karmic memory. Our potential of hidden creativity results from this karmic memory, which is found in the vibratory flow from the Throat Chakra to the Inner Eye Chakra.

For the purpose of personal meditation, the pure WHITE light should be directed to each of the seven major chakras in turn. Using the chakra color SKY BLUE for the throat, slowly and easily dwell on the chakra and visualize the color SKY BLUE as a fast-moving whirlpool Continue to do this till you find your point of focus in the center. You will know this when you see a bright SILVER spot that grows in the center of the vortex as the SKY BLUE energy circles faster and faster.

As the SILVER center starts to rise from the SKY BLUE chakra, begin to inhale deeply and slowly BRIGHT SILVER. As you exhale, feel and see the merging of the SKY BLUE and SILVER as they pull away toward the Inner Eye Chakra.

As the vibratory force picks up momentum, this SILVER and BLUE KARMIC THREAD will travel up to the Inner Eye. Continue to breathe easily until you have achieved this part of the exercise.

The end of the SILVER and BLUE cord is SILVER. Eventually, it will connect with your Inner Eye. You will recognize this occurrence when the SILVER point of the Karmic Thread merges into the beautiful INDIGO depths of the Inner Eye Chakra. Allow the SILVER and BLUE cord to penetrate this sixth chakra. The vibrant INDIGO of the Inner Eye will absorb and hold the Karmic Thread.

You have now connected the talents and abilities of your past-life efforts to your present-day creativity. Be still, very still, and wait till the karmic knowledge comes through the cord. As this occurs, you may have rapid glimpses of scenes from previous lives. Just relax until these settle down and you are presented with knowledge of your past talents and abilities.

# THE INNER EYE CHAKRA

The spiritual development of the INNER EYE Chakra can create vision on all levels. Also referred to as the Third Eye, the Inner Eye's symbolism has been used throughout time. Focus in this chakra area can stimulate all the other chakras. It is also known as the seat of paranormal powers.

Spiritual exercise in this area can increase inner vision and enhance the ability to meditate on many levels. Evidence of growth in this chakra is the ability to see beyond the emotional level, the gift of being truly impartial. You are able to observe your own life without emotion and to understand where you are on your path of destiny and what you must achieve.

The deep INDIGO tones of this chakra are unusually compelling, creating the need to study and apply your knowledge for the benefit of others. Once your inner vision is awakened, you will see color such as you have never before seen. You will possess love, compassion and balance which no one can disturb. You are destined to serve, and in knowing this you receive the gift of humility.

## THE CROWN CHAKRA

The CROWN Chakra is known as the Supreme Chakra. The life-giving power of your very existence emanates from this chakra. It is Spirit, it is complete and total Wisdom beyond the comprehension of man. Its pure cosmic vibrations have existed for all time. It is the Divine God Force that energizes the nature of man.

The very act of consciously breathing in through your Crown Chakra avails you of the God Force. Pure WHITE light mingled with GOLD represents the Crown energy. Breathing in through the Crown Chakra and directing the God Force throughout your physical body revitalizes and heals on all levels.

## EXERCISE 5: CLEANSING AND PROTECTION

Here is an exhilarating Esoteric Exercise—a breathing process that heals and protects. It is simple but most effecive.

1. Stand or lie with your arms raised outward and legs slightly apart.

2. Imagine the sphere beneath your feet. Hold that internal vision for a moment.

3. Now slowly bring your attention UP through the center of the body, breathing easily and naturally.

4. Your attention is on a straight GOLD line of energy.

5. When this GOLD line reaches the CROWN Chakra, exhale all negativity with your outgoing breath.

6. Focusing on the Crown Chakra, inhale slowly and deeply SILVER and GOLD energy through the top of your head.

7. As you bring in the energy with your breath, bring it straight DOWN to the sphere beneath your feet.

8. Exhale slowly, consciously bringing the SILVER and GOLD energy back up in a straight line to the INNER EYE. Release it, VISUALIZING THE OUTGOING ENERGY FORMING A PYRAMID WITH YOU AT ITS CENTER. Amen.

THIS BREATHING PROCESS WITH A CHAKRA FOCUS WILL RELEASE ALL EXISTING NEGATIVITY AND PROTECT YOU FROM ATTRACTING FURTHER NEGATIVITY. ANY TIME YOU WISH TO CLEANSE AND PROTECT YOURSELF, USE THIS SIMPLE, EFFECTIVE EXERCISE.

# CHAPTER 12

# CHAKRA COLORS AND HEALING

The mere activity of lifting your consciousness to a level of joy activates the seven major chakras. The ability to achieve this level is within each of us; it does not require a teacher or anyone but you.

Color, both seen and unseen, has a tremendous influence in your life; the various colors of the seven chakras affect every atom of your body. You can begin to understand the impact of these colors when you realize that every human being is like a living rainbow.

Let's review the seven major chakras and their respective colors:

## CHAKRA COLORS

| Number | Name | Color | Life Area |
|--------|------|-------|-----------|
| 1 | Root | RED | Foundations of life |
| 2 | Sacral | ORANGE | Life force |
| 3 | Umbilical | YELLOW | Personal power and courage |
| 4 | Heart | GREEN | Peace, balance and harmony |
| 5 | Throat | SKY BLUE | Creativity, karmic potential |
| 6 | Inner Eye | INDIGO | Spiritual wisdom and development |
| 7 | Crown | VIOLET | Universal concept |

Look at the color spectrum and what do you see? A rainbow, of course. Like the rainbow, each of us has the ability to transmit the perfect hues of nature. General stress causes an imbalance in the flow of these universal color energies. Self-imposed negativity adds to this imbalance. Particular stress factors are attracted to and ground themselves in the corresponding chakras. This situation can have an adverse affect on all levels—physical, mental and spiritual—in varying degrees.

## COLOR IMBALANCE

All of us are affected by color to some degree at all ages. Color imbalance is quite noticeable, especially where children are concerned. The first esoteric sign is a definite refusal to wear clothes of a certain color or a total dislike of certain rooms because of their color.

As always, you should not hesitate to call upon a medical doctor if there is a specific health problem involved. Esoterically, you can help the healing process and support the medication by recognizing the need for color balance. Alternate use of both chakra and Soul Colors* will help to assist esoteric healing and bring the colors back into balance.

It is important to note that a continuous focus on any one color is not advantageous. Too much color activity can overstimulate the natural vibratory flow in any one chakra. By alternating the color focus, using the Soul Color first, then the chakra color, you can limit the vibratory activity to its correct level. Using this alternate focusing procedure modifies the color intensity and neutralizes any excess. It can also increase the vibratory flow to the correct level, if needed.

## NEGATIVE EFFECTS ON FOUR LEVELS

Now let's examine the possible negative effects that could occur on the following four levels when your chakra colors become unbalanced:
PHYSICAL
MENTAL
SPIRITUAL
COLOR

*For an explanation of Soul Colors, which are determined by procedures in Gnothology, see: *The Connolly Book of Numbers, Vol. I,* Chapters 6, 10, 14; *Vol. II,* Chapter 3 (Newcastle, 1988).

## 1. Root Chakra

### PHYSICAL LEVEL

You would have a feeling of being deprived, of insecurity. You would tend to feel sorry for yourself, and your initial efforts in various areas would seem under constant threat. You might feel that you are unlucky, and your physical health may be unstable. You would be vulnerable to minor ailments and accidents.

### MENTAL LEVEL

You would feel inadequate and become concerned about your appearance, dress and general personality traits. You would also feel insecure socially, imagining yourself unable to cope and meet the standards of society.

### SPIRITUAL LEVEL

You would feel a sense of loss and a lack of direction. You would crave spiritual solace, yet be unable to evaluate spirituality in its proper context. You would find yourself seeking, attempting things, constantly making adjustments.

### COLOR LEVEL (RED)

On this level you would become involved in patterns of extreme behavior. You would be aggressive and overbearing at times. You might also be either overly competitive or totally withdrawn. An unbalanced Color Level would create unpredictable social and career behavior.

## 2. Sacral Chakra

### PHYSICAL LEVEL

A great deal of emotion would be apparent here—relationships must be strong to withstand this effect. If sustained, this imbalance can produce problems in this chakra region of the physical body, such as low back pain, or difficulties with the prostate or female organs. Children may resort to bed-wetting or a setback in toilet training.

## MENTAL LEVEL

Here you would experience constant friction in your close relationships. You would become unable to cope with intimate situations and become lost in the isolation of your own thoughts.

## SPIRITUAL LEVEL

You would seek to solidify deep spiritual philosophies and establish your spiritual roots. When challenged, you would become argumentative. You would explore alternate religious systems, but without satisfaction.

## COLOR LEVEL (ORANGE)

You would be overly dependent and quite demanding. Relationships could be severed with devastating consequences. You might become tearful and extremely emotional, overly sensitive to and aware of the opinions of others.

# 3. Umbilical Chakra

## PHYSICAL LEVEL

A child would display negative tendencies through unwarranted physical behavior, for example, becoming demanding, loud and boisterous. As an adult, you would also demonstrate the same signs of negativity. Incorrect use of Umbilical energy quickly shows in the personality as a lack of sensitivity and concern for others. Minor accidents and bruises could befall you and you could contract infectious diseases easily.

## MENTAL LEVEL

You would act before you think! Sometimes you might go to the extreme and become secretive and cunning. You could have great expectations and cause havoc when they are not realized. You could be unforgiving, and revenge would come easily. Secretly afraid, you would absorb energy from those around you.

## SPIRITUAL LEVEL

Ignoring what is, you would pursue what you think is possible to the detriment of all concerned. You might have a bombastic approach and a vivid imagination. You could be totally unrealistic, to the point where others feel it is a waste of time to argue with you.

## COLOR LEVEL (YELLOW)

You would project a strong feeling of agitation, nervous energy that is easily seen through. There's a lot of talk but no action. Like fireworks, you may seem brilliant, but the energy pattern will disappear quickly. Physical fatigue would occur more often than normal. You would become easily exhausted and disinterested. You would absorb energy from others and become quite self-centered.

# 4. Heart Chakra

## PHYSICAL LEVEL

You would feel discontented and greedy for love and attention. Acute sensitivity could be interpreted as a nervous condition. Inward stress could eventually focus into this chakra area, causing physical problems.

## MENTAL LEVEL

You would become critical, questioning the motives of others. Often you might experience a feeling of being threatened or overwhelmed. You could appear cold and aloof, with a continuous sense of anxiety.

## SPIRITUAL LEVEL

You could become a religious recluse, reluctant to share your beliefs because of an inability to trust. Fear could make you overly rigid regarding your faith.

## COLOR LEVEL (GREEN)

You would show a preference for dark or subdued colors in dress and decor. You would feel exposed or too noticeable with too much color. You might exclude yourself from direct social contact from a fear of direct confrontation.

The Heart Chakra is the fourth and middle chakra; consequently, it affects the balance of the upper and lower centers in the major chakra system.

# 5. Throat Chakra

## PHYSICAL LEVEL

You would have a low resistance to throat infections and could experience minor problems with eyes, ears and mouth. If there is any sense of feeling restricted, the negative energy will quickly affect these physical areas. A child might show resistance or experience difficulty in basic learning procedures.

## MENTAL LEVEL

You would be inclined to daydream about big ideas which are impeded by the inability to provide the necessary foundations for them. A constant sense of inner struggle would plague you. You would avoid important details and find it hard to concentrate.

## SPIRITUAL LEVEL

You would struggle to please, afraid to explore and go beyond traditional belief systems. You might have a tendency to become extremely emotional if your basic principles are questioned or challenged. You would feel compelled to resist change and would generally direct everything inwardly, causing a sense of heaviness in your personality.

## COLOR LEVEL (SKY BLUE)

You would experience a deep sense of loneliness. You might be moody and often depressed, preferring to stay home. Because of these tendencies, responsibilities would be ignored. You could become inept and lazy. Children will become untruthful in an effort to avoid exposure.

# 6. Inner Eye Chakra

## PHYSICAL LEVEL

You would become withdrawn and painfully sensitive. A fear of letting go, or of ridicule, could hide tremendous potential. Displaying negativity on this level often makes you a victim, and you become overly submissive. The first signs become evident when you endure humiliation and suffer without complaint. You would become vulnerable and try too hard to please.

## MENTAL LEVEL

You would feel inferior and unable to cope with abrasive situations. Retiring inward, you might show a great capacity for tolerance. Living in your own world, you would appear to be unaware of others taking advantage of you. You would make a constant effort to please, accepting conditions dictated to you.

## Spiritual Level

You would find much comfort in prayer. You would be supportive in order to avoid opposition. By accepting whatever comes along, you could eliminate any friction. The gentle aspect of this soul is easily overpowered when there is a deficiency in the chakra balance.

## Color Level (Indigo)

Indigo, with its varying shades of blue, would supplement the vibratory flow. A deliberate color exposure could provide the impetus required to reestablish the natural chakra balance. A serious and prolonged lack of chakra energy in this area would ultimately make you withdrawn and unsociable.

## 7. Crown Chakra

### All Levels

With this, the highest chakra, ALL FOUR LEVELS—Physical, Mental, Spiritual and Color (VIOLET)—are ONE. As the Crown Chakra is the source of entry and represents the pure collective universal energy, it constantly RECEIVES. This is the vital life force that fortifies the Etheric Body and in turn is used by the physical body.

# THE IMPORTANCE OF BALANCING THE CHAKRAS

This life-giving force flows through the chakra system. Our personal use and expression of this God Force is released continuously into the ether. Each soul emits an exact replica of who it is and what its karmic status is. This is known as the KARMIC IMAGE (see Chapter 13).

The soul extracts this vital life force and gives back individual and personal use of it. By this process you can see how your actions coalesce the energy back into the original God Force. In doing so you repeatedly imprint your personal growth and karmic progress into the Akashic

Records, which are the Astral memories of all events and every expression of man since the beginning of time. Once you have balanced your Crown Chakra, you have the remaining six major chakras to maintain in balance. The resulting energy constantly contributes to your Karmic Image. This record indicates the progress of each earth-life experience and then remains as a permanent spiritual record.

Imbalance of the Chakras reveals an imbalance in living. Either too little or too much chakra energy can be corrected by concentration and meditation. The use of color should be modified according to your personality traits, which can be self-observed through your inner motives and inclinations.

KARMIC STRESS OCCURS WHEN ANY OF THE MAJOR CHAKRAS ARE OUT OF BALANCE.

As you study the negative aspects of chakra imbalance, you may recognize within yourself where you need to apply some thought and planning. Generally speaking, you may discover that you have slight negativity in each of the chakra areas. Giving your attention to these areas will instantly promote healing.

Focusing too much or too little color on the chakras can create imbalance. Consequently, the ideal procedure is to create a steady flow of balance energies, using Karmic Meditation. This will ensure an even distribution of concentration. It will alert the conscious mind to reconsider habitual negative behavior patterns on all levels, which will result in the balance you are seeking.

The Karmic Meditation that follows is associated with the seven major chakras. Using them in meditation stimulates their energies, enabling you to reach higher levels of consciousness and giving you a deeper understanding of life and karma.

## MEDITATION 10: BALANCING THE CHAKRAS

This meditation is to help you balance your chakras and determine where there is imbalance. Daily use of this meditation can immediately create a feeling of well-being.

The procedure is given to facilitate regular use. I would advise that you wear WHITE, so as not to emphasize any particular chakra color. Lying on a WHITE sheet or towel will also help considerably. Another ideal situation would be to meditate while bathing. Water represents Spirit, so therefore a lack of color and the presence of water will provide the perfect situation for this meditation.

1. Reach up and out beyond any present conditions in your life. Leave behind any situation that is occupying your attention physically, mentally or spiritually. Know that you are going to place yourself in perfect balance. This is your intent.

2. Breathing easily and naturally, focus your attention on a sphere beneath your feet.

3. As you dwell on this area, the energy enters the sphere and becomes RED. Feel the RED under your feet. Wait till you feel the RED. . . .

4. Allow the RED energy to increase and bring your attention to the CROWN Chakra. As you do, feel it open gently, allowing a magnificent WHITE light to encircle the top of your head.

5. Gently alternate your focus between the RED sphere beneath your feet and the WHITE light encircling the top of your head. Wait until you can do this gently and easily, bringing your attention from your feet to the top of your head and establishing the RED sphere below and the WHITE circle above. . . .

6. Now you are ready to begin your SPECTRUM BALANCE. The RED sphere of energy gives a pleasant, warm glow beneath your feet.

7. Visualize breathing in WHITE light from the top of your head. As you inhale, bring the WHITE light gently down to the bottoms of your feet.

8. As you exhale, gently visualize the RED energy slowly entering your feet . . . your calves . . . your knees . . . your thighs . . . and into the RED ROOT Chakra.

9. Now, breathing easily, concentrate on the Root Chakra. As you do this you will activate it. It will begin to spin as it regains the correct balance. Relax and allow this to happen, visualizing the vibrant RED patterns of energy that extend brilliantly in front of your body.

10. Enjoy this activity, knowing that you are improving this karmic aspect of yourself. As the chakra spins, its speed will gently

erase your visualization and you will now feel solid and secure in the energy.

11. Now bring your attention up to the SACRAL Chakra. Visualize a small ORANGE disc below your navel. Allow yourself to hold this ORANGE energy and lift your attention again to the WHITE light above your head. Now easily and gently bring your focus to the Sacral Chakra and the ORANGE color. Then release it and focus on the WHITE light.

12. Inhale easily and gently from the Crown area and bring your breath to the Sacral Chakra. As you release your breath, feel the ORANGE energy building in the Sacral area. Continue to breathe this way through the Crown, bringing the WHITE light to the Sacral. As you do you steadily and easily inundate the whole area with a beautiful ORANGE color.

13. Now focus on the Sacral Chakra; as you do it will spin to its correct balance. Relax and allow this to happen. Visualize the bright ORANGE patterns of energy extending in front of your body.

14. As the spinning chakra builds its momentum, enjoy the activity, knowing that this karmic aspect of yourself is improving and correcting any imbalance here. As the spinning of the chakra apparently fades, your visualization subsides and you now begin to feel the solid ORANGE color firm and strong in your Sacral region.

15. Your focus now comes to the UMBILICAL Chakra. As you concentrate, the wonderful YELLOW energies begin to emanate. The YELLOW is clear and like the sun; rays shoot out from your focal point. As the energy increases, you can easily visualize the sun in the center of your body. Hold this image; now bring your attention to the WHITE light above the Crown Chakra.

16. Inhale slowly and easily, bringing the WHITE light into the Umbilical region. As it penetrates the chakra, feel the burst of YELLOW energy filling every cell within the chakra area.

17. As you release the brilliant WHITE energy, you feel its comfort and beauty. You now focus on the spinning YELLOW chakra. See the exquisite formations of light and color as the

chakra accelerates. The continual bursting of YELLOW energy is providing you with spiritual strength.

18. When the Chakra appears to subside, bathe yourself in the YELLOW healing vibrations. Relax and enjoy this for a few moments. Wait. . . .

19. Gently lift your attention to the HEART Chakra. As you do this, feel the contrast between the warm vibrancy of the YELLOW and the coolness of the GREEN. It feels good. Let the GREEN spread to every part of the chakra region. Let all tension flow away as the GREEN energy touches every cell.

20. Holding the GREEN, now lift your attention to the WHITE light above your Crown Chakra. Feel yourself rising up and inhale this WHITE light, bringing it directly into the Heart region. As the WHITE light touches this chakra area, see it become more brilliant. See it quickly spread out to all cells, flooding them with the true GREEN chakra color.

21. As you exhale, the chakra maintains the GREEN vibratory flow. Now focus on the Heart area and see the chakra spin all the many shades of GREEN. Spend some time enjoying this activity. The rapidly changing GREENS encompass every part of the Heart region.

22. Be aware of the esoteric control you now have. Let your senses feel the impact of the balanced chakras. You are now in the center of your chakra system. Feel the essential difference between the lower and upper parts of your body. How solid and secure the lower, balanced chakras feel in contrast to the upper chakras, which are still waiting.

23. You are now anxious to go up to the THROAT Chakra. Bring your attention to the WHITE light above the Crown and inhale deeply and easily. Bring the WHITE light to the Throat Chakra. Immediately you will feel the keen SKY BLUE color rapidly extending to every part of this chakra region. When you exhale, the Throat Chakra begins to fill up with the vibrant SKY BLUE energy.

24. Relax and allow the SKY BLUE vibrations to touch all the vital areas. Feel this energy fill up your mouth, bathing your teeth, tongue and gums. Bring the energy to the back of your throat

and swallow THREE times. Let the SKY BLUE rays now enter your ears and balance your hearing. Bring them up to your eyes and allow the rays to cover them completely. These strong, keen vibrations heal and improve your senses as they spread into every part of this region.

25. Bring your focus now to the Throat Chakra and feel the increased energy as it begins to spin. Like a fragrant shower, the SKY BLUE energy is once again touching the whole chakra area. Feel the thrust of the chakra spinning in front of your throat. Allow your physical body to sag and totally relax.

26. Once again you go up to the Crown Chakra and deeply inhale the WHITE light. Release the WHITE light into the INNER EYE Chakra and become aware of the beautiful INDIGO color here. It is serene and peaceful. Relax and feel this deep INDIGO, concentrating on your Inner Eye.

27. Now begin a new breathing pattern. Inhale WHITE light through your Inner Eye. Release this breath in INDIGO directly through the Inner Eye. The method of breathing is IN through the Inner Eye and OUT through the Inner Eye. Breathe in WHITE—breathe out INDIGO. Do this in a relaxed and easy manner. Enjoy the fullness, the sense of upper balance, as you breathe in this way.

28. As you continue to breathe in WHITE and out INDIGO, you will feel the intensity of the Inner Eye Chakra spinning rapidly. Your focus in this chakra region is twofold: 1) It expels all negativity and arouses the wisdom at the root of the chakra; 2) The force of the spinning chakra clears negativity in your aura, thus giving you a feeling of stability and purpose.

29. As the visualization subsides due to the rapid movement of the chakra, relax for a few moments and enjoy the feeling of balance. Wait. . . .

30. Now lift your entire attention to the WHITE light above your head. As you breathe in to the Crown Chakra, keep this intake of breath from expanding into other areas. Limit the intake by breathing in shorter breaths, filling only the top of your head— the upper Crown. This will necessitate your breathing out

quickly. Follow this procedure: BREATHE IN WHITE AND BREATHE OUT VIOLET—THREE TIMES ONLY.

31. CONSCIOUSLY RELAX AND FEEL THE VIOLET RAYS FLOOD THE CROWN CHAKRA. BREATHE EASILY AND NORMALLY. YOU NEED ONLY THREE BREATHS TO CONCLUDE THIS MEDITATION.

32. As you relax in the VIOLET rays, be aware of the comfort and revitalization that is now entering your body. As the VIOLET energy subsides, it spreads gently throughout the body. You are now totally immersed in VIOLET. Enjoy this level until it subsides. Wait. . . .

33. When the VIOLET energy fades away, inhale THREE breaths of WHITE light and exhale THREE breaths of WHITE light. You have now concluded the SPECTRUM MEDITATION for balancing the seven major chakras.

NOTE: Your thoughts and ideas following this meditation can be quite innovative. It is good to have writing materials available to jot down any information received.

Repetition of this meditation eventually will produce an "esoteric X-ray" effect! It will bring you to a personal conscious level where you can observe the areas of your life that you can improve. Spiritual exercise, like physical exercise, improves the areas of concentration. This is why I suggest writing materials be available. When this exercise is conducted in a group, the collective notes will provide material for a worthwhile group discussion.

CHAPTER 13

# THE KARMIC IMAGE

Who and what you are can be disguised socially, but when it comes to karma, this cannot be done. There is no fooling your karmic destiny. As you exist in body, mind and soul, you draw your energy from the Universal Source. Upon extracting this energy, you use it according to your needs as determined by the conscious level. The way in which you use this energy is based on your conscious needs. These actions in turn affect your subconscious and Higher Conscious levels, which are receptive to them. How you use the energy is automatically transmitted to the higher levels.

As the resulting energy patterns are transmitted through these levels, the original energy forms a picture of who and what you are. This image reflects the karmic structure of your soul at the present time. Your Karmic Image is imprinted upon the ether and becomes a part of the eternal Akashic Record.

This record is not unlike a movie, in that it has a beginning, a middle and an end. However, unlike a movie, you can consciously change your "story" if you wish to. It is possible to become a different person, but you must go beyond the mere intent to do so. You cannot go on indefinitely just having good intentions without putting these intentions to work.

Your Higher Self experiences stress when it is exposed to activities not previously planned for this particular lifetime. You feel this stress! The Higher Self appeals to your conscious level; you can recognize this message through what we term our conscience. Unfortunately, the conscious level has some measure of control and can resist the Higher Consciousness. This is done quite often, so you learn to either follow your conscience or ignore it and persuade yourself that your actions were justified. Since these excuses are not acceptable to the Higher Self, you may consciously derive some satisfaction from feeling that the world is against you.

You can fool the world, you can fool yourself, but *not* the Higher Consciousness. You enter this life to improve *all* levels of your consciousness.


## LOVE AND THE KARMIC IMAGE

When all three levels of consciousness are working toegether, you experience joy. The ability to love is a part of this joy. People who are devoid of love feel a constant lack, an emptiness. Feeling this way eliminates motivation and creates a terrible sense of loneliness.

Love is the essence of the universal energy. As you receive this energy, you have the desire to share it with other human beings. Under normal circumstances it is first activated on the parental level. A child normally receives love initially from the parents. If for any reason the child does not experience love, obviously its life foundations will be affected. Nevertheless, through growth and development, you learn to experience love on many levels. The lack of a specific love relationship does not necessarily mean that you are deprived of love.

Each human being is constantly receiving love. Correctly used, this love is first directed to your self. In doing this you learn self-respect, for without self-respect you are not processing the universal energy correctly. Perhaps it is being diverted in some ways: undesirable relationships, bad habits, self-pity. Considering the ample flow of this energy, you can see that regardless of any present circumstance, you can redirect your thoughts and change your application of love. Lack of self-love creates lack of luster. Your Karmic Image is projected from who you are and what you are, so when you are down there is only one place to go and that is *up*. You should not be concerned as to *how* you get up but *when*. During my many years of counseling I have discovered that when a person realizes it is now time to change, to do something else, they often become befuddled and have no idea where to start.

## CORRECTING YOUR KARMIC IMAGE

To correct your Karmic Image you must begin with *yourself*. Let go of your hurts—the pains of past relationships, the terrible career disappointments. All the sources of previous dilemmas must be released entirely. This can only be accomplished if you believe in yourself, believe you can begin again. Another you, the real you, the you that is *really* you is possible.

Begin your focus by looking at everything around you. For example, see how you have allowed things to deteriorate. Neglecting your home or appearance are the first signs. No matter how distressed you feel, attend to these things. Set a deadline—a date to begin and a date to finish. After you have made this effort, you will feel much better and find yourself in improved circumstances.

That was the hard part! It's always difficult to start a new project, especially when you have no interest in it. But your interest will increase with each effort you make. Faith is the chief ingredient, faith in yourself. You'll like the initial results of your first efforts. Liking the results will make you like yourself for the effort you made. This is the beginning of love. Pleasing yourself regardless of yourself.

As you continue to apply effort toward yourself, it will reflect in everything you say and do. From this point your life will improve and you will begin to gain a deep sense of personal satisfaction. During this whole process you will be improving your attitude, which will improve your relationsips with others.

To increase your energy and improve your general outlook, you can begin to meditate. Regular periods of meditation will provide wisdom and personal growth. Your focus will enlarge and you will improve on all levels as you create good spiritual, mental and physical behavior patterns.

## USING FAITH FOR PERSONAL POWER

First, let's analyze lack of control and how you unwittingly produce energy for this situation. Control is first issued via the universal energy directly to the Higher Consciousness. As it transfers to the conscious level it is bombarded with conditions that are not conducive to its purpose. There is a power available on all levels of consciousness which is a vital and necessary force. This power is faith.

When you hear the word "faith," you are immediately reminded of religious convictions. Faith is an unquestioning belief that does not require proof or evidence. The strength of true faith is the real foundation of success on all levels. But faith can be activated only if practiced. This requires self-recognition followed by an unbending purpose and a vigorous effort toward particular personal goals.

Using faith correctly is the secret key to producing results. Many people have a very careless attitude toward faith. Not placing much value on what they give, they expend faith in various empty causes. The end result if usually one of disaster or bitter disappointment. Investing your faith in the actions of another can be a deliberately passive act which denies you its fullest use. This is not to say that it is wrong to have faith in another. What *is* wrong is giving your fatih indiscriminately: for example, relying on another to extricate you from your responsibilities. Having faith in someone else can often be translated as, "I am passing my responsibility to you."

Simple words do not provide the fiber and substance of true faith. Saying "I love you" and then having faith that the other person loves you in return trivializes faith. Another example might be, "Oh, you'll do it, Jean, I have faith in you." First of all, when you realize what has been said, you know that this statement means little or nothing if you are speaking generally. What is really meant, perhaps, is that you are depending on Jean to accomplish a task simply because you know you can't or won't.

What is real and meaningful in your life? Placing faith in well-established relationships and ventures is good. But do you realize how little faith you use? This powerful force exists constantly, yet on a day-to-day basis it is normally not even recognized, let alone used. It is saved and given only in certain extreme circumstances.

In your lifetime you have probably experienced an emotional upset when the faith you invested in someone was betrayed. This is normal and acceptable. The true difficulty arises when you refuse to reinvest your faith. After undergoing such disappointment, you are naturally disinclined to extend your faith again. You dwell on your shattered memories and refuse to extend any further loyalty, feeling that your belief system may be proven wrong once more.

The ultimate secret is to establish faith in *yourself!* Beginning with self-adjustment and the ability to establish exactly what you want solidifies the essence of faith. In turn, your faith will grow and mature. Obstacles will be removed as a result of this powerful force. Difficulties will be overcome and you will find that miraculously, you have the strength to maintain yourself.

Your personal faith can manifest your greatest desires. Faith is not a dreamlike substance—it is actual power. It is a force that is touched only by your goals! It is your permission to your Higher Consciousness to focus totally on your intent, without doubt or fear. We are referring to the universal energy, which is allowed to function without reservation and manifest your needs.

Faith needs a purpose to achieve success. Opportunity is important to success but of no value alone. You must invest further energy. How is it possible to go through life avoiding success? One word is the answer: EXCUSES. Even at an early age children can quickly find excuses for doing things they shouldn't. We soon become skilled at using excuses to release ourselves from obligations, yet this does not lead us to the success we desire.

The need, the challenge, the drive are all negated as we skillfully manipulate ourselves on the racecourse of life. Self-adjustment and the ability to establish exactly what you want solidifies the essence of faith. To adjust, you must reconsider your karmic path. If there is an overwhelming disappointment in your personal achievements, then it is obvious that your Higher Self knows better. Tapping the wisdom of the Higher Self is definitely related to self-adjustment. If you are unable to tune in to your karmic ideals, if you feel cut off from your Higher Self, then the need to readjust becomes vital to your karmic purpose. The way you have been going obviously is not correct for you. Perhaps it is too easy or perhaps you prefer to rely on others. The answer is for you to make an immediate self-adjustment. The pieces *will* fall together. Feeling awkward initially is to be expected. Whenever you change a way of doing things, your brain is still geared toward the old way through years of practice. But the new way will eventually become normal, and the power of faith will project you toward success in achieving your goals.

Faith is not a dream, it is a realistic approach to achieving the happiness and balance required on your karmic path. Remember, don't think of success in terms of the number of opportunities presented; think of it as an opportunity to be recognized before it is too late. The next step is being ready to act upon the opportunity, with faith in it and in yourself.

If you lack confidence, then perhaps you also lack faith. If you feel that you have confidence but no faith, then your confidence is *not* confidence. Examine which level of energy you are using. Showing confidence in a "sure thing" is comparatively easy. Confidence is a firm belief in your own ability. Being overly confident is allowing the ego to participate. True confidence is the outward sign of faith. This faith is directed inward toward your own success and goals. It does not require approval or acknowledgment from others. Faith is a quiet, powerful force that clears the way for the karmic traveler. It is the resulting energy of the conscious mind accepting the wisdom of the Higher Self and using this wisdom to learn ultimate control for personal power. As long as you invest your energy in true faith, you need not endure the pain of Karmic Stress.

## MEDITATION 11: ACHIEVING ULTIMATE CONTROL

To gain ultimate control, you must first relinquish your present control. Begin by allowing yourself sufficient time to relax physically, mentally and spiritually. A WHITE candle helps to eliminate any resistance you may have.

Light music played softly may assist your relaxation procedure. Be sure you are not feeling tired. It is important that you be alert and ready to contribute toward this exercise.

Remove everything that may impede your meditation. Tight clothing, jewelry, shoes, hairpins, belts, etc. To ensure that your exercise is uninterrupted, attend to all possible outside interference: telephone, pets, children, etc.

1. As you begin to relax, become conscious of your body weight. From the top of your head to the tips of your fingers and toes, feel the fullness of your physical body.

2. Enjoy this procedure; it is very relaxing and will help you to reach ultimate control. Allow plenty of time to relax. Wait. . . .

3. As your body now becomes fully relaxed, focus your attention approximately three feet in front of your body. As you concentrate your focus in this one area, wait until your CONTROL GUIDE appears.

4. As you wait, repeat THREE times:
   I AM READY TO EXPLORE THE PATH TO MY ULTIMATE CONTROL.
   I AM READY TO EXPLORE THE PATH TO MY ULTIMATE CONTROL.
   I AM READY TO EXPLORE THE PATH TO MY ULTIMATE CONTROL.

5. When the Control Guide appears, step forward and give thanks.

6. Look down at your feet and see the rough path. See the stones and the dust. Now look straight ahead and see the rocky terrain. Extending your inner vision, see the boulders you will climb. Absorb all this and consider the purpose of your journey.

7. When ready to proceed, acknowledge your intent to your Control Guide. The Guide will now extend a special blessing which you will see and feel as WHITE light. Breathe in this WHITE light deeply and slowly. As you exhale, your Guide will begin the journey.

8. You will see a lack of vegetation. The ground appears barren and dry. Ask your Guide why this is so.
   Wait. . . .

9. Absorb the wisdom you receive and continue on your journey. The trees have no leaves. Listen to the wisdom of your Guide as the reason for this is explained to you.
   Wait. . . .

10. You are traveling along your own path. There is no sign of life or activity. You are going back through past failures. As these failures reveal themselves to you, acknowledge each one in turn but do not dwell upon them. Your Guide continues to walk and you must follow.

11. As you approach the boulders, your Guide will begin to climb. Follow his footsteps. Each foothold is a crevice of past errors and mistakes. As you reach for consecutive footholds, you are reminded of your past negativity.

12. You see your Guide reach up his arms as the climb becomes steeper and more severe. As you follow, keep your eyes focused on the Guide as he climbs.

13. The Guide does not disturb the loose rocks. It is clear where he has placed his foot. Continue to climb and follow in his footsteps. Be aware that you yourself are responsible for the falling rocks behind. Know that each step you take is for the purpose of conquering your past dilemmas.

14. Around your waist is your Emotional Belt. Through your efforts to climb beyond your present problems, the belt becomes tighter. Grip a hand on the rock above and untie your Emotional Belt.
Wait. . . .

15. As the belt is loosened, you feel new energy surging within you. Your Guide is now farther ahead. He looks back and smiles. Continue your climb. As you reach for a hidden crevice of past hurts and pain, you lose your shoes.
Wait. . . .

16. Your Guide turns again and asks you to continue. He tells you that the shoes were old and worn and no longer useful for your new path.
Wait. . . .

17. Inhale a deep breath of WHITE energy and lift yourself UP, UP, UP. The sheer boulder is now difficult to climb. Look up once more and see your Guide offer his hand.
Wait. . . .

18. As your hands connect, you instantly experience an exhilarating energy. You feel exceptionally light as the strength of your Guide now pulls you easily to the top of the boulder. You are now lying on the top. You can feel the softness of grass under your body.
Wait. . . .

19. You know that you are now gaining new strength. Every part of your body is receiving WHITE light.
Wait. . . .

20. You gradually become aware of sounds. Listen.
Wait. . . .

21. Your Guide now asks you to stand up and look straight ahead. Before you is a beautiful path. There are other souls walking toward you, smiling and radiant.
Wait. . . .

22. The Guide now asks you to turn around. You are poised on the edge of the Cliff of Your Past Errors. As you look down, it is steep and forbidding. It is difficult for you to realize that you have made this personal climb. It is dark and cloudy, and you do not like what you see.
Wait. . . .

23. Your Guide now touches your arm and asks you to walk into the new, untouched future. He will present you with future possibilities and show you the resulting joys.
Wait FIVE minutes. . . .

24. Now continue to walk on your path. You feel good and are ready to follow the Guide to a beautiful pool on the LEFT. Your Guide asks you to gaze into the pool and see your new reflection.
Wait. . . .

25. You are excited and pleased by the vision presented.

26. The Guide now takes you to a pool on the RIGHT. It is stagnant and unmoving. As you look into this pool, you see yourself devoid of control. You are shown exactly what to expect if you continue on your present course.
Wait. . . .

27. Now anxious to leave, you look at your Guide, who smiles gently and points to a glistening WHITE tower. You know this is the Tower of Ultimate Control. Your Guide leads you to the entrance and will wait till you return.

28. As you enter the tower, you are surprised to see such neglect. It is such a contrast to the outside. You see a narrow staircase winding upward. You feel compelled to climb it. As you climb, you know it is imperative to look up and leave the past behind.
Wait. . . .

29. The higher you climb the easier it becomes. You now see your

Higher Self waiting at the top—a healthier and happier you smiling and giving encouragement as you finish your climb. Wait. . . .

30. Arriving at the top, you are surrounded by great and beautiful vistas. Each way you look is magnificent. You feel invigorated and excited. Your Higher Self clearly reveals all that can be yours.
Wait. . . .

31. You now become aware that you need the gift of FAITH before you can contribute your energy to all these wonderful possiblities. Ask your Higher Self for FAITH. Now see your Higher Self take off the Robe of Radiance and give it to you. Wait. . . .

32. Now turn and go back down the stairs. Waiting at the tower entrance is your Guide. Begin to walk back over the lush countryside. Your heart is now filled with joy and anticipation. As you reach the edge of the cliff, you see the forbidding, barren landscape and the steep cliff descending before you.

Your Guide now asks you to put on the Robe of Radiance. As you do so, EVERYTHING BEFORE YOU BECOMES BEAUTIFUL AND POSSIBLE. The landscape is now new and exciting. The cliff of despair is now rolling hills of green. Your Guide asks you to wear your Robe of Radiance, which is your new FAITH, for all to see. Wear it with courage and persistence. He now says good-bye. Give thanks and lie quietly for a while in your radiant Robe of FAITH.

CHAPTER 14

# DESTINY AND FREE WILL

Each of us has an individual Path of Destiny predetermined by the soul to achieve our karmic goals. But within this path, we have the gift of free will. This gives us the opportunity to explore our destiny and examine its purpose and potential. When we fully understand this, we can experience karma without stress.

## YOUR PATH OF DESTINY

Once you have the above information planted firmly in your mind, you can begin to formulate a plan based on your Path of Destiny. Think of it as a journey:

PATH OF DESTINY   =   A Major Freeway
FREE WILL         =   Motels, Cafés, Gas Stations, etc.
POINT OF DESTINY  =   Chicago

Imagine you are traveling by car from your present location to a large city—say, Chicago. You begin your trip with a specific destination in mind. This is your Point of Destiny, the place where your destiny is fulfilled. Free will comes into play as you choose which of many motels, cafés, gas stations, etc., to stop at and patronize along the way. There are many to choose from, but only you make the choice. Where, when and for how long are yours to decide.

No matter how long you stay off the freeway, sightseeing or visiting, sooner or later you must resume your journey. Free will considers the trip as a whole, so your decisions must be made accordingly. Your final destination—"Chicago"—and time of arrival do not change. Your choice of your own personal route does not affect your Point of Destiny.

The Higher Consciousness—your Higher Self—knows your Path of Destiny from beginning to end. It knows where and when your Point of Destiny awaits you. Your conscious mind exercises your choices as free will, but is not privy to the information stored in the Higher Mind concerning your future. Your subconscious mind keeps a constant record of your every thought, word and deed, from the moment of birth until you have completed your Path of Destiny.

You have the power to access all *past* records of this life, and your Higher Consciousness has access to all experiences in your previous lives.

If the subconscious becomes overloaded with negative experiences, it becomes somewhat isolated. This hinders the Higher Self, so that you are not always able to communicate freely with it.

When this lifespan is over and you are ready to go into transition, you are presented with the activities recorded on your subconscious level. There are many personal experiences on record relating to death or transition. There are souls who did not go through transition completely but survived to relate "near-death experiences." Although their personal stories may differ, they all have one important thing in common: They were confronted with a rapid but vivid image of how they lived.

This is why I referred to the subconscious as a recording instrument. It is switched on at the moment of birth and continues to make a record of your entire life. It would appear that the subconscious has to release this energy prior to transition. I'm sure that you don't particularly look forward to an "instant replay," but I do know that through meditation exercises, negative information can be erased before it's too late. The practice of meditation alleviates inner pressure and reduces Karmic Stress. Also, we find that the Higher Self can impregnate the conscious self in a positive manner.

## RELEASING NEGATIVITY

It is said that "confession is good for the soul." In this modern day we can use the "release" as well. Regular meditation creates the energy required to release all previous negativity—known and unknown, seen and unseen. Three little words—"Release, Release, Release"—can give you the keys to personal freedom. Allow your conscious mind to release on a daily basis. Then follow through with your meditation practice, and the results are astounding! You will immediately begin to feel the pressure leave. Your mind will expand, and you will feel the personal freedom that was restricted by your Karmic Stress.

By the act of releasing, you trigger the esoteric mechanism that controls the three levels of consciousness. In the act of meditation you have the ability to transform what has been and what is into a solution of what will be. Do you realize that there are people walking this earth who have simply no control? No understanding of these principles? They believe in something called "fate," which after all is just another word for Destiny. Believing that fate rules your life suggests that there are no alternatives. The essential ingredient of free will is commonly overlooked or ignored.

You can express your free will *now* and begin to let go of all past negativity. Assert yourself and see yourself actually in command, through the sensible process of release.

If you concentrate on the word "release," you begin to consider new outlets of personal expression. In the act of letting go, you are confronted with space! All the things you would like to do become possible simply because you have created space in your levels of consciousness. The inability to plan ahead, think and cope is a result of storing old, negative cells.

This reminds me of a story regarding my parents. My mother had an attachment to her treasures—old letters, and Christmas and birthday cards. Throughout the years she never quite knew where to store all these things. My father suggested that everything be put in a box and sealed. If at the end of six months there was no reason to look in the box, or Mother was unable to remember what she had stored in the box, then it would be ridiculous to continue storing the contents. I can still hear my mother's voice saying, "But what will I do with the box?" My father answered, "Throw it away."

It is easy to see a parallel with this story and your unwanted, unneeded memories of past negativity. The only difference is that you don't have to wait six months to throw them away! You don't need them, you can't remember every detail, you don't have a reason to remember if they are long gone. Pack them all in a Box of Determination. Toss in painful childhood memories and anything elese that you can live without. When this is accomplished, THROW AWAY THE BOX!

The following Karmic Meditation will help you initiate this process. It may take more than one box! Each time you sense an unexplainable negativity, start to pack another box and use the following meditation exercise. As you discard each box, you are making a determined and positive effort to rid yourself of Karmic Stress.

Before using the meditation, however, let me give you another Esoteric Exercise to help you consciously focus on releasing all negativity, known and unknown, seen and unseen. During the day, from time to time allow your conscious mind to release as often as needed. Don't waste energy by trying to focus on deatils; just put your attention on the releaseing process itself.

You may prefer to make a physical gesture or a verbal statement of your releasing. This will make the release more meaningful to your conscious mind, but it is not at all necessary. Your conscious effort to release is instantly recorded on the subconscious level.

## EXERCISE 6:  NEGATIVITY RELEASE

1. Stand in front of a full-length mirror with your hands open, palms up. Look directly at your reflection and say: RELEASE, RELEASE, RELEASE.
2. As you walk during the day, without lifting your arms, open your hands and stretch your fingers wide, saying firmly: RELEASE, RELEASE, RELEASE.

This kind of approach is ideal and prepares the conscious mind for the releasing process of meditation. This premeditative exercise should be done on a daily basis—it's a wonderful habit to acquire. Do it while you shower in the morning or before going to bed. This activity informs your conscious mind that you are no longer willing to store negative energy patterns.

All levels of consciousness penetrate every aspect of your being. When you make a deliberate effort to release all negativity, it leaves the subconscious and is brought up to the conscious level. The final point of exit for this negative residue is through the pores and other outlets of the physical body. Therefore, showering or bathing after this meditation is an excellent idea and will complement your meditation.

## MEDITATION 12: RELEASE AND RENEW

1. As you relax, see yourself in a bright YELLOW robe, eager and ready to accomplish spiritual work.
   Wait. . . .

2. Looking straight ahead with your inner vision, see the vast countryside. It is brown, with little or no growth. The sun is shining and you are waiting to start your personal journey.
   Wait. . . .

3. As the sun shines overhead, look to the sky immediately before you. You are waiting and looking for a PURPLE SPHERE. Soon you begin to see it in the distance.
   Wait. . . .

4. The PURPLE SPHERE becomes larger and larger as it approaches. You are feeling anxious and ready to begin your spiritual journey. The nearer the SPHERE comes the larger it gets. It is huge, magnificent and PURPLE. Now watch it descend. See how gently this enormous SPHERE comes to earth.
   Wait. . . .

5. Feel in your heart the depth of wisdom this SPHERE of PURPLE brings. Where the sun touches the PURPLE, you see a radiance of color that is breathtaking. Watch the colors and feel the energy of wisdom pulsating within the waiting SPHERE.
   Wait. . . .

6. The time is ready for you to prepare. Look at your YELLOW robe and begin to breathe in YELLOW through the UMBILICAL Chakra. Now exhale YELLOW through the INNER EYE in a relaxed and easy manner. As you continue this YELLOW breathing process, feel strength and power surrounding you.
   Wait. . . .

7. Now continue to breathe normally and see the brilliant YEL-
   LOW rays extending toward the PURPLE SPHERE. When your
   YELLOW radiance touches the PURPLE SPHERE, wait till you
   see the doors open and a PURPLE light form a path toward
   you.
   Wait. . . .

8. This is a beautiful sight and you feel eager to step forward. You
   are waiting for your MASTER to come to the open doors.
   Wait. . . .

9. As your Master comes into view, walk toward the PURPLE
   SPHERE. It feels good; your robe of YELLOW is radiant. As
   you walk nearer to the PURPLE SPHERE, you are now ready
   to expel any remaining negativity. Be aware of the YELLOW
   around you. Be aware of your strength and power. As you
   reach the doors of the PURPLE SPHERE, say:
   I CONSCIOUSLY USE MY PERSONAL POWER TO RID
   MYSELF OF ALL NEGATIVITY, KNOWN AND UNKNOWN,
   SEEN AND UNSEEN.

10. Feel all negativity leaving you. Feel your strength increase. As
    your Master smiles, step forward into the PURPLE SPHERE.
    The doors close behind you and you are now in brilliant
    WHITE LIGHT.

11. Go to the CENTER of the SPHERE and greet your Master. Feel
    your Master's warmth, wisdom and love.
    Wait. . . .

12. Your Master takes your hands and you feel the SPHERE begin
    to LIFT UP. It continues to lift slowly. You are very aware of
    the ascending vibrations. Your Master holds your hands as the
    speed increases. You are going UP, UP and UP. The WHITE
    light is moving rapidly as the SPHERE climbs. You see the
    universal SILVER energy merging with the brilliant WHITE.
    As you travel higher and higher, you feel far away from all
    concern or worry. Your negative vibrations cannot exist on this
    level. Your Master smiles as you begin to understand.

13. You now feel the speed decrease. You feel the PURPLE
    SPHERE come to a halt, slowly and softly. The doors open

once again. Before you is a complete vision of all that you have experienced in this life. There are voices, sounds, people. You have been brought to the level of your SUBCONSCIOUS. You have absolutely no fear. Your Master asks you to step out and see the many reasons for your dilemmas. You are asked to bring back ONLY the situations you want to keep. Your Master will wait in the SPHERE. Step outside and immediately feel the difference in temperature. The doors of the PURPLE SPHERE are now closed until you return. Walk into your past. Visit any aspect you wish. Bring back only what is good and leave the rest behind forever.
Wait. . . .

14. You are now ready to return to the PURPLE SPHERE. Walk to the doors and they will open. Your Master greets you with an embrace. You are happy to be back. The Master now asks what you have brought back with you. Relate everything that is important and precious enough for you to retain.
Wait. . . .

15. Your Master now asks what you have discarded. Feel your Master take the weight of your subconscious from you.
Wait. . . .

16. Now look at your YELLOW robe: it is soiled and dirty. Your Master takes you to a beautiful room, which is yours. He leaves you. Remove your soiled robe. Beyond the room is the Pool of Tranquility. Bathe in this soothing, relaxing pool. Allow the GREEN of the water to soak into every pore. Enjoy this, for you are in your very own place.
Wait. . . .

17. Step out of the Tranquility Pool and go back to your beautiful room. On the bed you will see a new YELLOW robe embroidered in GOLD. Sit in the GOLDEN chair you see and the Master will enter, asking whether you have totally released your negativity. Answer. Now follow the Master to the center of the PURPLE SPHERE. Sit with your Master and ask for wisdom.
Wait. . . .

18. Once again you feel the vibrations as the PURPLE SPHERE starts to descend. The Master holds your hands, and you feel the energy change rapidly. As you feel the PURPLE SPHERE gently land, the doors open once again. Say good-bye to your Master and give thanks. Listen to the last words of your Master. Wait. . . .

19. As you step out of the SPHERE, the countryside is exquisite. There are trees, birds, many flowers and many colors. The sun is gentle and your YELLOW robe is again brilliant. You feel refreshed and full of new energy. Lie down in the shade and give thanks for this beautiful spiritual experience. Wait. . . .

20. Think of all the things you considered precious—the situations, relationships and memories you wished to retain. Contemplate the wisdom received and how you can immediately apply it to your life.

CHAPTER 15

# ESOTERIC CALISTHENICS

Whenever we talk about exercise, we think of diets and health clubs and sports and jogging. The focus is on the physical body—how it looks, how it feels, how it works. Naturally, a reasonable amount of physical exercise and a proper diet, preferably one supervised by your doctor, are good for you. People of middle age and older should also consult their doctors about the kind and amount of exercise they take.

Have you ever noticed the difference between a young child and an adult as they exercise? The adult concentrates inwardly, the focus being entirely related to the body. A child has an air of sheer joy: the arms move as if reaching for a rainbow; the legs appear to dance. The child is thrusting outward from a pure center unencumbered by karmic baggage, healthy chakras bubbling and spinning and causing the face to reflect the inner strength. A child appears to be painting a picture with every outward movement. The conscious level is reaching out and mingling with the Universal Vibratory Force.

The difference between the child and the adult is mainly in the focus. The adult focuses inward, the child outward. This nonphysical, concentrating aspect of exercise is the part we may call ESOTERIC CALISTHENICS.

The word "calisthenics" comes from the Greek *kallos* (beauty) plus *sthenos* (strength). Through the practice of calisthenics, we can reinforce and replenish the vital energy we know as life. Calisthenics is simply an organized, regimented method of exercising various parts of the body. But the very idea of such a determined method of exercise makes many of us tense and tired. The only saving virtue is the hoped-for reduction in poundage when we look at our scales at the end of the week.

Esoteric Calisthenics are a different matter. They can strengthen and maintain your life force without exhausting or frustrating you. It all begins with attitude. First, you must erase all ideas of what you normally think of as exercise. The next step is to understand how Esoteric Calisthenics work and what kind of results they can produce for you.

## THE IMPORTANCE OF INTENT

The foundation of Esoteric Calisthenics is INTENT. Your intent is to achieve a spiritual balance within your physical body. This intent must come from the proper source, which in this case is the CONSCIOUS MIND. Without pure intent flowing from the conscious mind, you cannot reap the therapeutic advantages of Esoteric Calisthenics.

Practicing Esoteric Calisthenics is another way of increasing your vibratory rate and eliminating Karmic Stress on a day-to-day basis. Children can also benefit from this system, as the Emotional Level releases tension and fear. When my children were babies, I introduced them to Esoteric Calisthenics and they enjoyed every minute of it. Remembering the delight they showed, when my grandchildren arrived, I also used the system with them. I was pleased to see that the generation gap did not lessen the fun and joy of these new little exercisers.

To practice Esoteric Calisthenics, you must not associate the physical movements with the normal method of exercise. So if you happen to enjoy physical exercise, consider this system a separate activity.

Let your conscious mind absorb the simple esoteric theory of the system, which is composed of two important concepts:

1. INTENT
2. CONSCIOUS APPLICATION OF INTENT

Your intent is to improve your physical equilibrium, which in turn controls your inner balance. You want to open yourself to universal energy through physical movement. A child in one of my classes once remarked that she felt as though she were taking a spiritual shower. This delightful image is not far from the truth. Every esoteric scholar knows that as we release, we are replenished.

Although physical movement is required, it is not necessary to exert yourself. For this reason, senior citizens will also enjoy working with Esoteric Calisthenics if their health allows. Where there is a need for healing, a medical doctor should of course be consulted, but esoteric healing can be applied simultaneously with medically prescribed healing. Practicing Esoteric Calisthenics is more of a preventive measure anyway.

## TWO TYPES OF ESOTERIC CALISTHENICS

You will need sufficient space to move about. Doing the exercises outside is a wonderful experience, as the exposure to fresh air gives you a great feeling of exhilaration. But be aware, however, that you should not exercise outdoors if the air quality is unhealthy, as it is in many major cities.

This esoteric "tune-up" is invigoration; many people find that even facial features develop a more youthful glow if the exercises are done on a regular basis. As long as you remember your intent, you will benefit in many ways.

There are two types of Esoteric Calisthenics. You may choose to perform them either way, or alternate both methods:

1. VISUAL CALISTHENICS
   You begin with visualization, then perform the physical exercises.
2. PHYSICAL CALISTHENICS
   You do the esoteric exercises only, without the visualization.

I have found that both children and adults usually seem to prefer to include the visualization. They enjoy working in the Garden of Calisthenics. If you prefer to conduct the calisthenics without the visualization, merely follow the physical movements.

Music is both soothing and helpful when played softly. The rhythm of the music can actually dictate the pace of the exercise, allowing for natural expression.

Remember that all calisthenic movements should be graceful, flowing and easy, as in Tai-Chi Ch'uan. Remember that your INTENT is consciously to release all negativity from every part of your body, yet KNOW that all the energy will be replenished.

Before beginning your Esoteric Calisthenics, which will be given on the following pages as Karmic Meditation 13, it is helpful to make a verbal statement of your intent:

> I AM CONSCIOUSLY RELEASING ALL NEGATIVITY FROM EVERY PART OF MY BODY.
> I KNOW THAT I WILL BE REPLENISHED.

## MEDITATION 13:  THE ROSE—VISION AND MOVEMENT

After the basic preparation procedure, close your eyes.

1. VISUALIZATION: Visualize yourself in a lovely garden. This is the Garden of Calisthenics. See yourself surrounded by beautiful roses of many different colors. Imagine soft GREEN grass beneath your feet. Now imagine that YOU are an exquisite ROSE, all curled up into a bud. As you begin your exercise, each hidden petal of yourself is wrapped tightly over another. Inside your ROSE self is a magnificent perfume waiting to be released.
Wait. . . .

2. EXERCISE: As the music begins, gently close your hands; then slowly and gracefully allow each finger to uncurl, exposing your palms.
Wait. . . .

3. EXERCISE: Now gently turn your palms over and slowly stretch every finger and thumb. Do this THREE times.
Wait. . . .

4. EXERCISE: Rotate your wrists slowly and let your hands make a circle. Do this THREE times.
Wait. . . .

5. EXERCISE: Softly push your hands forward, fingers spread and palms outward. Do this THREE times.
Wait. . . .

6. EXERCISE: With hands touching, slowly raise your arms. Then separate the hands and allow the arms to come back to the side of your body. Bring the RIGHT arm forward with hand open, fingers spread, and allow the arm to drop slowly as it comes back to the body.
Wait. . . .

7. EXERCISE: With hands touching, again raise your arms slowly. Separate the hands and allow the arms to come back to the side of your body. Bring the LEFT arm forward with hand open, fingers spread, and allow the arm to drop slowly as it comes back to the body.
Wait. . . .

8. EXERCISE: Very easily, without any strain, move your head from side to side. Gently raise your head and look at the sky or ceiling above you. Then gently lower your head and raise it slowly again.
Wait. . . .

9. VISUALIZATION: You are the center of the ROSE. Everything you are is tightly enfolded in the bud. Feel the urge to unfold.
Wait. . . .

10. EXERCISE: Using very little effort, stretch out your arms. Count THREE and let them curl back to your body. Reach out again with both arms, and as you count to THREE, feel the summer breeze ripple around you.
Wait. . . .

11. EXERCISE: Lift your LEFT leg just a little and slowly thrust it out away from your body. Count THREE and let it return. Then lift your RIGHT leg a bit and

thrust it out away from your body. Count THREE and let it return.

Wait. . . .

12. VISUALIZATION: Now bring your attention to the center of the ROSE. Focus deep inside the bud. Feel every part of you reducing down to a dot of pure WHITE LIGHT. This WHITE light is the original essence of the flower. It is a tiny speck of pure untouched energy that is about to manifest itself as a ROSE. Dwell on this beauty and remain deep within the bud. Fill your consciousness with the Divine Light and allow the pure Original Plan to flow into your stream of consciousness.

Wait. . . .

13. VISUALIZATION: As the intensity builds, feel the urge to expand this WHITE light. Feel the urge to spread the petals that hold your light. Let the energy of pure desire build into your light till every breath becomes pure expectation.

Wait. . . .

14. VISUALIZATION: All you need now is the power of the SUN to penetrate you. Anticipate the power of the sun trying to reach you.

Wait. . . .

15. VISUALIZATION: You begin to feel the sun's warmth. Your protecting petals appear to quiver as the sun's rays reach down toward your light.

Wait. . . .

16. VISUALIZATION: Expand your light by inhaling a slow, deep YELLOW breath. Retain this breath for the count of THREE. As you release the breath, feel your inner desire to blend with the sun and complete your Original Purpose. Do this once again.

Wait. . . .

17. VISUALIZATION: As you focus now on the universal WHITE light deep within, be aware of the incoming force. The rays of the sun are now finding your Universal Center. Breathe easily and allow inner growth and expansion. Realize that as light meets light, nature is now transforming all that you are.
Wait. . . .

18. VISUALIZATION: Watch with your Inner Eye and see the universal WHITE light now become a center of GOLD deep within your rosebud. The energy growing within you is like a rising sun. Each breath you take begins to form a GOLDEN SPHERE directly in your center.
Wait. . . .

19. VISUALIZATION: Every part of your being is waiting to unfold. As the GOLDEN energy solidifies, the need to OPEN is felt in every cell of your being.
Wait. . . .

20. VISUALIZATION: It is time! You are now ready to manifest. Your original essence has been transformed. Gradually the rays of the sun subside. Feel the energy lessen. The GOLDEN energy is throbbing with joy. Look out now. All about you is velvet BLACKNESS, studded with millions of stars. You know that you are ready to become the OPEN ROSE, but you must wait a bit longer. Bring all your energy back to your center and wait. . . .

21. EXERCISE: Obey the urge to curl back up into a tight bud. Let your legs bend and draw them up to your body. Bring your arms in as you bend your back. Roll gently on your side. Let your head fall down toward your chest. Close up tightly. You are now in the fetal position, waiting to be born.

22. VISUALIZATION: Tiny specks of early dawn light are now dancing all through your body. You absorb this
energy and transform it into the joy of NEW
BIRTH.

23. VISUALIZATION: You can feel the warmth of day trying to give
life to every part of your body. The desire to
become the OPEN ROSE and give to life the essence of who you are is now becoming stronger
and stronger. You are beautiful, you are vital,
you are a part of God's creation. It is time to
understand this wisdom and to recognize what
you must give to the world. Think about these
things; consider how the light and joy now
waiting deep within you can be manifested.
Think about how you can touch the lives of
others, the many things that can be changed
through your new birth. Think about all these
things as the sun prepares its energy for your
rebirth.
Wait. . . .

24. VISUALIZATION: Listen! You can actually hear the sounds of life:
the movements of birds, the flapping of their
wings, their chattering as they greet the new
day. This is your day. You are going to be a
part of all that is out beyond you. You are
conscious now of YELLOW light all around you.
Breathe in through the UMBILICAL Chakra a
bright GOLDEN YELLOW. As you release the
breath back through the center, you feel a
tremendous urge to OPEN and stretch. It gov-
erns every atom of your existence. Capture
once more the delight, the beauty and internal
purity of desire and intent.
Wait. . . .

25. EXERCISE: It is time! SLOWLY uncurl. Feel the release and
joy of true rebirth. The light instantly hits and
you must adjust.
Wait. . . .

26. EXERCISE:    As you become adjusted, you are now ready to live! You are ready to express all the love and beauty of your Original Plan. Now all your limbs enjoy the stretching. Reach out to the light of day. From the center of your body, everything is OPENING and STRETCHING. Every internal organ is opening to the new light. As you rebirth, you are born in perfection. Stretch every part of your body—fingers and toes. Let every cell of your body be exposed to the new light. Breathe in this new light. Because your intent comes from the universal light, LET LIGHT TOUCH LIGHT.
Wait. . . .

27. EXERCISE:    Your body continues to move slowly and easily. It stretches out as the light washes over you. You are rebirthing, you are being renewed, you are anticipating new life. Allow every muscle to move and stretch. Concentrate on exposing every part of yourself to the new light. Enjoy and bathe in the beauty of new birth.
Wait. . . .

28. VISUALIZATION: Feel every atom of your being drenched in the light that surrounds you. See and feel your whole body pulsating with the pure vibratory flow of health.
Wait. . . .

29. VISUALIZATION: You are totally relaxed and continue to stretch easily. Each movement you make opens every vital organ of your body to the light. You are drinking the pure essence of life and vitality.
Wait. . . .

30. VISUALIZATION: Extract EVERYTHING you need from the light. Fill yourself completely with the living force of the universe.
Wait. . . .

31. VISUALIZATION: You are reborn! You have transformed the seed into living beauty. You have used the power that is yours. Lift your head gently and feel the rays of the sun. Now bring your attention to the results of your effort. You are as a ROSE. You are perfect, you are beautiful. You will be the source of joy for many. As many souls touch your life, they will inhale the pure fragrance of your true essence. Sense the joy of your new responsibility. THINK OF WHAT YOU WILL DO.
Wait. . . .

32. VISUALIZATION: You are what you think. Think only good things. Life is waiting for you and you are ready for it. Live it well.
WHAT COLOR ROSE ARE YOU?

33. EXERCISE: Contemplate what you have experienced for a few minutes, then open your eyes and record your experience.

## THE GIFTS OF YOUR ROSE

The color of your rose is very important to your esoteric understanding of this meditation. Don't be surprised if the color changes each time you conduct the meditation. Sometimes it will remain the same during a particular cycle in your life, then change color when a new cycle begins. For more about life cycles and color in relation to them, see *The Connolly Book of Numbers, Vols. I and II* (Newcastle, 1988).

The rose is a gift to you from your Higher Self. It is colored by your Master. The color reveals a gift of added energy which you need at this time. It changes to match your current need.

As you contemplate your meditation, let your thoughts dwell on the color of your rose. Think about how you can use this gift from your Master immediately and give thanks for it. The color of your rose represents the intensity of your Master's gift. Different colors and shades indicate various qualities and blessings. Deeper shades show that additional strength is being imparted to you, possibly over a longer period of time. Lighter shades mean that you should use the gift in moderation.

## Red Rose

The RED rose is a beautiful gift of Individuality. You have the personal power to take charge of your life. You possess the ability to be yourself and establish your views in a balanced and harmonious way. You could receive recognition and respect. You may also have the opportunity to express your abilities and leadership potential.

## Orange Rose

The vibratory influence of the lovely ORANGE rose will attract new people into your life. It will help you solve any existing difficulties with relationships. The shade of ORANGE determines the nature of the relationship. A perfect ORANGE rose could mean joy and happiness for you and another.

## Yellow Rose

Ideas and plans will be inspired. You will discover new outlets of self-expression. The vibrant YELLOW rose is full of creative energy. Your Master wants you to look ahead and see the happiness and joy that can be yours. Previous obstacles will be cleared from your path. Take a new look and a new approach and success will be yours.

## Green/Blue/Indigo/Violet Roses

Roses of these colors promise change. New life cycles are directly ahead and old cycles are ending. Some area of your life is going to change for the better. Your Master's gift is to encourage you to anticipate this event. It will happen very soon, so discard old, worn-out emotions and be ready!

## Pink Rose

Your Master has given you an earthly gift. You are entering a new cycle of success. The measure of this success is indicated by the shade of PINK. The radiance of the PINK rose is now attracting the success you need. Put everything in order and be ready for new situations and unexpected events.

## Gold Rose

You will soon experience a sudden surge of energy. You will be looking in many directions. This is a karmic gift and will open a new vista in your life. Your reluctance to change will be challenged by new and exciting possibilities. You may feel overwhelmed, but you should be confident and allow your basic instincts and faith to guide you.

## Silver Rose

The SILVER rose brings the gift of healing for yourself and others. Explore ways you can develop and use this wonderful gift. Your Master will extend his love and power so that you can use this vital energy. As you accept this energy, you will also receive healing in all aspects of your life. You will feel the desire to teach; wisdom will be given to you when you are ready for this spiritual gift.

## White Rose

The WHITE rose is a very special gift that brings wisdom. You will feel the urge to study and acquire esoteric knowledge. Your past talents will surface as you search your levels of consciousness. The purity of the WHITE rose is a great blessing from your Master, giving you inspiration and the ability to discover your karmic talents. You will receive support from a higher level. Don't hesitate, for you and yours will benefit greatly from your efforts.

## CHAKRA CALISTHENICS

As you progress with your Esoteric Calisthenics, you'll find that your knowledge of chakras will help you considerably. Knowing where your chakras are located and being familiar with their colors will allow you to release your negativity. This is the sole purpose of Chakra Calisthenics. They are not intended to enhance spiritual development through activation of the chakras.

In the following Esoteric Exercise, the conscious mind focuses on the intent of releasing. This focus is projected out and away from the body, beginning with the hands and gradually moving into every area of the body. The idea is to focus externally *and* internally at the same time. It is a slow, deliberate scan that surveys the entire body. In return, as each part of the body is consciously scanned, holding the intent, it then releases any negative factors there.

Perusing the entire body is enhanced by music, which provides an excellent background. If you are in a class led by a teacher, you can follow the procedure as a group, everyone focusing on the same physical area at the same time. The teacher can make pertinent remarks relating to each area and remind the class of their intent.

Releasing existing negativity should reveal the cause, which is the real reason for your stress. Chakra Calisthenics attempt to expose the cause of your negativity. Once the negative factors are located, acknowledged and understood, then, depending on which level the negativity was located, you can determine the best physical action to take.

With the chakra system, all the exercise is done within the body; no physical movements are used. INTENT and FOCUS are the two tools you employ, turning all your attention inward to each chakra region. Repetitions of this exercise will fortify your inner balance.

## EXERCISE 7: SCANNING THE BODY

1. Begin with a statement of your intent, either aloud or mentally: I AM CONSCIOUSLY RELEASING NEGATIVITY FROM EVERY PART OF MY BODY. I KNOW I WILL BE REPLENISHED.

2. Visualize a reflection of yourself standing before you.
   Wait. . . .

3. Focus intently on your reflection. Look beneath your feet and see a SPHERE of vivid GREEN energy.
   Wait. . . .

4. See the GREEN energy rise and go into the ROOT Chakra. As the GREEN touches the chakra, it bursts into brilliant RED light. At the point of contact, feel the rush of RED energy circulate throughout the chakra area. As you feel the rush of RED, you also see it in your reflection. Reaffirming your INTENT, SEE the RED become clearer and clearer. FEEL the RED totally filling the Root Chakra.
   Wait. . . .

5. Looking at your reflection, now see the SACRAL Chakra filling up and spreading throughout its area with a brilliant ORANGE. Feel the force of the Sacral energy as it spreads out and completely fills the chakra.
   Wait. . . .

6. Your physical body can now feel the increase of energy. The brilliant ORANGE feels good and stable. Feel the roots of the RED and the firmness of the ORANGE.
   Wait. . . .

7. It feels good to see your reflection now adjusting to the positive chakra energy. See a burst of YELLOW as you look at the UMBILICAL Chakra. See how it rapidly covers the complete chakra area. The beautiful, warm YELLOW envelopes the chakra. As the energy increases, you feel the power building in your own physical body.
   Wait. . . .

8. As you gaze at the beauty of the YELLOW chakra in your reflection, your body feels as though it is expanding. Allow this to happen and enjoy the sensation of fullness.
   Wait. . . .

9. The YELLOW subsides and appears to solidify in both your reflection and your body. Now you see the relaxing GREEN

pouring into the HEART Chakra. It is a wonderful experience. Great peace is now entering your heart. As you see the GREEN spreading its tranquility throughout the Heart Chakra area, you feel a deep sense of tranquility there.
Wait. . . .

10. Watch the GREEN travel down your arms and into your hands. See your heart protected and balanced as the GREEN continues to flood the chakra area. A deep sense of peace now enters your entire physical body. Your heart is drenched in true tranquility. As the GREEN now touches every living cell, you feel blessed and fortified. A new spiritual strength comes into your heart and you recognize your needs.
Wait. . . .

11. In your reflection you now see SKY BLUE energies encircling your THROAT Chakra. The sparkle of this energy is like SILVER flecks darting in the SKY BLUE. The energy covers your face. Your eyes, ears and skin are all touched by the vibrancy of the SKY BLUE. The Throat Chakra spins and you see the SILVER touching and cleansing, releasing all negativity.
Wait. . . .

12. As you watch this beautiful sight, your Throat Chakra begins to activate. You feel exhilarated as the SKY BLUE energy now fills every cell in the chakra area. Let it circulate and establish perfect balance.
Wait. . . .

13. In your reflection you now see deep INDIGO swirling around the INNER EYE. The chakra begins to spin, and you see the center of the energy as it goes back into the Inner Eye. The INDIGO spreads throughout the chakra regions, and you sense the wisdom available.
Wait. . . .

14. As you look at the Inner Eye the INDIGO energy now comes toward you. As it touches your brow, you feel it surging into your head and alerting your center of wisdom. Breathe in a little deeper to absorb the energy now coming into your Inner Eye Chakra.
Wait. . . .

15. A VIOLET light now is touching the CROWN of your reflection. Your reflection looks perfect. All the chakra colors are clear and vibrant. See your reflection in this perfect balance. STEP FORWARD INTO YOUR REFLECTION and feel an immediate increase of inner power. Feel the merging of all the vibrant colors.
Wait. . . .

16. You now feel the VIOLET in your CROWN Chakra. You are glowing; your radiance extends and fills everything that you are.
Wait. . . .

17. Your body is inundated with light. You feel as though you are in the center of a star. Every part of your mind, body and soul is now activated as your radiance merges with the Universal Light. You are in command, you are in control. YOU HAVE FOUND YOURSELF.

## ON THE PHYSICAL LEVEL

Any pain or disorder recognized on the physical level needs the attention of a medical doctor. Exercising with Physical Calisthenics in a painful area is obviously not the thing to do! The immediate cause of discomfort or pain is usually understood. Although there is a measure of negativity associated with the location of discomfort, other esoteric healing procedures would be more suitable. Contributing healing energies along with medical attention can accelerate the healing process.

If you have no physical health problems, then you can enjoy Physical Calisthenics to rejuvenate the body. They will regenerate the vibratory flow and eliminate any pending negativity caused by stress on the other levels.

Chakra Calisthenics are ideal if there happens to be a physical disability. The secret of Calisthenics in any form is your INTENT:

I AM CONSCIOUSLY RELEASING NEGATIVITY FROM EVERY PART OF MY BODY. I KNOW I WILL BE REPLENISHED.

# CHAPTER 16

# FINDING A PLACE OF YOUR OWN

Most of us spend too much time in situations and places that are not to our liking. We may say we are bored, or we can't stand it, but nevertheless, we go to these places and do these things we dislike for various reasons: habit, loyalty, financial dependency, lack of will, etc. Often we put up with people and places we hate out of fear that change will be worse than the present, fear of the unknown.

Human beings can be quite accepting of misfortune. History has recorded many instances of courageous souls who, even in extremely painful circumstances, have demonstrated a patience almost beyond comprehension. Some have displayed incredible courage and strength while enduring great pressure and fear.

A case in point is that of the great Spanish writer, Miguel de Cervantes (1547–1616), who managed to write the first part of one of the world's most enduring masterpieces, *Don Quixote*, while in prison.

When the conscious mind has a choice, it can choose to succumb to an experience or transfer it directly to other levels of consciousness. This power exists within all of us. It is used to varying degrees every day.

Sometimes we can be quite amazed by our resilience. The mind is far-reaching: if it has a reason to tolerate something, it will provide the staying power. This unique energy is not a reserve to use in an emergency; it is always available. Today we are so closely monitored that we learn at an early age to respond "correctly," regardless of how we actually feel. A sense of duty prevails.

Words like "loyalty" and "responsibility" motivate our efforts. These qualities are admirable, but only if we actually feel the loyalty, only if we really accept the responsibility. Wonderful, inspiring courage is also often seen with a mother and her children. In her daily routine, love and patience are demonstrated on a regular basis. So too with the father, tolerating a crushing work schedule to pay the mortgage, buy food and clothes, etc.

Every day, every hour, someone somewhere is a hero. They go beyond what is expected. Our heros are of all ages and live on every part of this planet. For many it is a quiet endurance. In the depth of despair there are many silent heroes. Perhaps you are one of these. Maybe you have come to the conclusion that there is no other way— your Path of Destiny is difficult. Well, take heart—there is a place to go!

## A PLACE TO GO

It isn't necessary to travel on a bus or fly to some exotic island. You have a place to go, both physical and esoteric. When you stretch your conscious level to the limit under emotional pressure it becomes practically impossible to avail yourself of your higher energies. Even under these circumstances, you will have a place to go.

Think for a moment of the places that really give you a feeling of pleasure and security, no matter how limited you may feel. These places are like small cameos and can go unnoticed by the conscious level because of anxiety and stress. Bring your thoughts in and try not to include the whole picture. Think of a few minutes rather than a week. Leave your present difficulties on the outer fringes of your consciousness. Draw in close and discover your place to go—a place where you can relax for short periods and forget about your troubles. It's not very far away. Let me give you a few examples:

1. Your favorite room
2. A quiet place in the park
3. A coffee shop
4. Your back yard
5. A short walk around the block
6. Your church
7. Browsing in a book store

8. Your favorite chair
9. Watching children playing
10. The beach, mountains, a museum

These are places where you can forget all your concerns for a short while. You will find these small indulgences worthwhile and beneficial. Simple activities that give simple pleasures can take you away from boring and repetitious routine.

Instead of always doing the usual, do something unusual. Escape for short periods. Do it as often as you can. A half-hour away from your fixed, mundane schedule will lessen the energy you release emotionally. The excuses I've heard are all the same:

1. I don't have enough time.
2. I don't know where to go.
3. I don't know what to do.
4. I can't do that.
5. It's not worth the time.
6. It won't change anything.
7. How can I do that?
8. It won't work.
9. How can that help? Etc., etc.

The above statements are not true. They are merely excuses. Once you resort to excuses, you are surely in a rut. It is only by making the effort to include different activities in your life that you can begin to change your routine. We all have the time; we may not want to use it differently, but we do have the time. We do have places where we can go and relax.

Break your routine and see what happens. If you have somewhere to go and something to do, you will start taking a new interest in yourself. The minute this happens you begin to rid yourself of Karmic Stress.

## THREE LEVELS OF CONSCIOUSNESS

If you cannot talk yourself into getting out and going to a physical place to relax, there is still a place for you to go. You can escape *anytime* into your own Inner World—your esoteric place.

So if the pressure of work or other duties prevents you from physical release, take a few minutes and discover your esoteric place. It is a place of peace and serenity. It will heighten your senses. There are colors and laughter, sunshine and flowers. The moon and the stars are the brightest you have ever seen them. You will always look and feel your best. It is your place and only love exists there. It is a beautiful place to go.

As you know, your mind operates on three levels of consciousness, each of which has a definite function:

1. CONSCIOUS              Current thoughts
2. SUBCONSCIOUS           Storage of memory
3. HIGHER CONSCIOUSNESS   Supreme wisdom of soul

Allowing your imagination to work for the purpose of releasing pressure can incite positive new thoughts. Acting on these new thoughts can bring you to a Place of Possibility.

Flying in an airplane high above the clouds, you are exposed to unusual beauty. Everything seems clear and pure. You could quite easily think you were in another world. The light has its own spectacular effect. Below, there is a soft, deep carpet of clouds. But then, you may see turmoil—dark, threatening colors invading the placidity. The clouds churn, creating a forbidding scene.

You see what looks like the core of a terrible atmospheric distur- bance. You anticipate disaster and wonder what it must be like on the freeways now. Is everything all right at home? You consider all the pos- sible problems that could result. You realize that it's going to be a tough trip for those who are going to pick you up at the airport. Then you smile inwardly, for you know that regardless of weather conditions, there's going to be much happiness when you embrace your loved ones. Wind, storm or snow cannot touch or destroy the joy of anticipating the union.

The picture I have given you could easily represent the three levels of consciousness. The Higher Consciousness watches all that is happen- ing below but cannot assist unless recognized and called upon.

The clouds of turmoil are the subconscious; ordinary life as we know it, the world we live in, represents the conscious level. The air- craft represents your own private jet: each morning when you awake you prepare for the landing. You descend from the higher atmosphere and brace yourself for the turbulence. As you cut through the swirling fears, you are once again reminded of things done and not done. Your seat belt holds you tightly in situations you must face. The alarm clock rings and pierces your ongoing fears. The landing is one of desolation, but immediately the conscious level adjusts and supplies the same old excuses, the same old reasons. You submit to routine and once more you are on the ground, trying to find your way through your everyday life.

Getting in touch with your Higher Consciousness means accepting the higher wisdom. Perhaps this is exactly what you would like. To do this you must submit to the higher level and let go of preconceived ideas. This is not easy, but when you realize that without this wisdom your plans never seem to materialize, you have an ideal reason to open up to your Higher Self.

What is seldom understood is that when you do allow the Higher Self to gain control, your conscious mind works even better. You begin to operate at a higher energy level. Thoughts become actions and actions bring long-awaited results. The reason it is difficult to let go is because you are not sure that anything else exists beyond your present conscious thinking capacity.

The Higher Consciousness remains intact by its very nature. Pure cosmic energy activates the Higher Self. In doing so it allows wisdom to flow in from the God source continually. Man has a power which he uses expertly as a child, but he often loses it as he matures. This power is the imagination. Think of this as an elastic wall around your conscious level. When you are really forced to think and solve problems, you venture near this fringe area.

Children are much bolder. They run to the fringe and stretch it out as far as possible. Its elasticity allows them to expand and explore beyond the normal thinking process. If you would think of the elastic fringe and press hard against it, you would see life entirely differently. Everything would seem kinder and more possible. Yet the conscious mind avoids this experience for fear of the unknown.

Only by pushing yourself to the outer fringe and stepping beyond it will you see the brilliant light of wisdom shining from the Higher Consciousness. This is your esoteric place to go.

## MEDITATION 14: YOUR INNER PLACE

As you relax and unwind, feel the desire to stretch beyond your normal thinking pattern. Don't exert any tension. With eyes closed establish a sense of knowing. KNOW that there is a level of light which can change your whole life.

Let go of your tension. Let your arms and legs fully relax. Feel a deep urge to travel beyond your conscious barriers.

1.  See yourself as a child about six or seven years old. You are alone in a garden and feeling very happy.
    Wait. . . .

2.  You have no concerns. You are anxious to explore this beautiful garden. There are so many brightly colored flowers. See how many different kinds of flowers you can find. Don't be afraid—you are quite safe. The sun is shining brightly. How many different kinds of flowers can you see?
    Wait. . . .

3.  Look at the trees. See how low the branches are. You can even see places where you could climb very easily. See which tree you would like to climb. Find one with a nice thick branch that you can sit on so that you can see everything in the garden. Go ahead, climb up. When you're on the branch I will come and talk to you.
    Wait. . . .

4.  So here you are! Do you like being a child? does it feel good? Relax for a moment. I want you to take a good look at your hands. Now look at your shoes and socks. What clothes are you wearing?
    Wait. . . .

5.  What is your name? Do you like your name? Who is your friend? Remember my questions and you can tell me later. Look up into the tree. If you listen carefully you can hear baby birds. You can hear the rustle of wings as the mother bird flies into the nest. Now look over the big garden and all the paths and flowers.
    Wait. . . .

6.  Listen again! Can you hear water bubbling from a fountain? Look again at the garden and you will see the fountain. Climb down from your tree and go to the fountain and you can drink. Go now. Take a drink.
    Wait. . . .

7. Are you refreshed? Now we will walk on the pathway, past the flower bed full of RED flowers and over to the WHITE fence. As soon as you get there you can sit on the fence and wait for me.
Wait. . . .

8. Isn't this garden lovely? You like it here, don't you? This is your garden and you can come here any time. As you sit on the fence, let's take a look at the field on the other side. It's just a big, open field. It has no pathways, no flowers, just hedges and trees around the sides. Now pretend you are an artist. This large field is your canvas. You can paint whatever you please. Let's fill it with lots of color and all kinds of wonderful things. Color me in first on the other side of the field and I will watch you paint.
Wait. . . .

9. Our next game is going to be fun. Everything you've painted is now coming to life! Watch it carefully and see what happens.
Wait. . . .

10. Now climb off the fence and walk through your picture over to me. Take your time and look around at everything you drew. Enjoy yourself. I will be waiting on the other side of the field.
Wait. . . .

11. Now come and sit with me on the fence. If you look over to the left you will see a beautiful palace with a GOLDEN road.
Listen . . . it has started to rain, we must hurry.
Feel how the wind seems to push us back.
The clouds are black and stormy.
The rain is so heavy we can hardly walk.
We want to reach the GOLDEN road.
It has become very dark and we can't see very well.
It feels like we are climbing a steep hill.
The wind is making a loud noise.
It would be nice to be home in a warm bed.
LOOK! There's a bright light ahead and now it isn't raining anymore.
The wind has stopped, the sun is shining.

You feel happy again.

You have a friend, your MASTER, waiting for you. Your Master will show you all the marvelous things you can do. See yourself, you are now grown. You are now YOU. You have important things to hear and important questions to ask. Sit with your Master and receive the wisdom given you. But first . . . ask your Master's name.

Wait a few minutes. . . .

12. Now it is time to go. You are anxious to record all that you have learned. Bow your head and give thanks. As you raise your head you will see yourself back in the garden, but now you are mature. Light surrounds you and you are ready to apply the wisdom to your life.

13. It was good being a child. It was good to go beyond your imagination to the Higher Consciousness. Now you are free to be who you really are.

14. Gently relax; when you are ready, record your experience.

# CHAPTER 17

# CYCLOTONES

Opposing any negative force requires strength and concentration. Inevitably you will become tired and try alternate methods. You also waste a lot of time doing this, and the combination of lost time and wasted energy creates a great deal of Karmic Stress. These periods of frustration prevent you from progressing in life. But if you fully understand the unique complexity and rigidity of your existence, you can overcome apparent obstacles.

In my previous books on Gnothology, an ancient form of numerology, I have gone into considerable depth regarding the various life cycles which are reflected in a personalized chart.* In this book I would like to introduce a new concept, which I call CYCLOTONES.

A cyclotone is a specific period of time governed by a universal influence. Your karmic entry was predetermined according to the complexity of the heavens. The nature of the Cyclotone provides the vibratory aspect required by the soul to achieve its unique destiny. This karmic entry is then affected by a complex arrangement of personalized Inner Cycles.

Each of these cycles is equally important. They have a precise link that provides information concerning the individual purpose of your life path. Through a serious study of Gnothology it is possible to delineate this knowledge and achieve limited predictions about the probable

*See: *The Connolly Book of Numbers, Vols. I & II* (Newcastle, 1988).

future by interpreting the sequence of cycles and correlating the timing process.

The overall energy of the Cyclotone extends its vibratory power to all resulting cycles. The potency of the Cyclotone conducts the rhythm of the consecutive cycles. If you are attuned and sensitive to the input of the Cyclotone, you create harmony within your Inner cycles. This level would then be considered Cyclotonal. Think of the most positive situations that have happened in your life, the times when you experienced the supreme level of joy, or a perfect memory. You experienced a Cyclotonal effect.

A Cyclotone is a PERSONAL cycle. The day you were born is the first day of your first Cyclotone. With skill in Gnothology and astrology you can see the governing and predictable possibilities. But a positive forecast might not be as great as you anticipated. Although your Inner cycles are favorably aspected, the measure of success depends on the compatible vibratory influence of the Cyclotone.

## DELINEATION PROCEDURES

1. A Cyclotone is a period of 52 DAYS.
2. Each Cyclotone connects its influence directly to a chakra during each designated period.
3. The color of the Cyclotone is identical to that of the corresponding chakra.
4. Each Cyclotone commences at the date of birth and therefore is designated a personal cycle.
5. There are SEVEN Cyclotones each annually, thus giving a total of 364 DAYS.
6. On January 8 of each year ALL Cyclotones are WHITE. On this date there is a universal oneness. Gnothologically, it is the first day of the new year.
7. As the vibratory power of each Cyclotone impacts and merges with the chakra, it has an immediate effect. This starts to diminish on the 50th day of EACH Cyclotone.
8. These three last days—50,51 and 52—are the RENASCENT PERIOD. During this time you are susceptible and open. You can easily be influenced.

9. Under the influence of each Cyclotone, energy levels change, affecting health, occupation and general outlook. The Renascent Period should be used to adjust to the incoming Cyclotone and release the outgoing one.

10. The Renascent Period should be a relaxing time. Try to plan your activities accordingly.

## CYCLOTONES AND BIRTHDAYS

In order to understand the influence of the seven Cyclotones on your life cycles, you need to understand how they relate to your birthday. The following procedures will show you how to calculate your Cyclotones.

There are two days during each year which are different from the other 363. Birthdays which fall on either JANUARY 8 or FEBRUARY 29 (Leap Year) have a universal aspect. These birthdays always have the high influence of the color WHITE. When counting the 52-day segments of each Cyclotone, if your birthday falls on January 8 or February 29, do NOT include your birthday in the count. This does not lessen the vibratory impact; instead of experiencing the effect of the Cyclotone immediately, you enjoy an esoteric high by spending your birthday on the WHITE level.

Here's how to calculate your Cyclotones:

## WHITE Level Birthdays

### JANUARY 8 BIRTHDAY                                          WHITE

| | | | | | |
|---|---|---|---|---|---|
| Jan 9 (Day 1) | through Mar 1 | (Day 52) = 52 Days | = Cyclotone 1 = | RED |
| Mar 2 (Day 1) | through Apr 22 | (Day 52) = 52 Days | = Cyclotone 2 = | ORANGE |
| Apr 23 (Day 1) | through Jun 13 | (Day 52) = 52 Days | = Cyclotone 3 = | YELLOW |
| Jun 14 (Day 1) | through Aug 4 | (Day 52) = 52 Days | = Cyclotone 4 = | GREEN |
| Aug 5 (Day 1) | through Sep 25 | (Day 52) = 52 Days | = Cyclotone 5 = | SKY BLUE |
| Sep 26 (Day 1) | through Nov 16 | (Day 52) = 52 Days | = Cyclotone 6 = | INDIGO |
| Nov 17 (Day 1) | through Jan 7 | (Day 52) = 52 Days | = Cyclotone 7 = | VIOLET |

## FEBRUARY 29 BIRTHDAY                                                WHITE

| | | | | | | |
|---|---|---|---|---|---|---|
| Mar 1 (Day 1) | through Apr 21 | (Day 52) = | 52 Days = | Cyclotone 1 = | RED |
| Apr 22 (Day 1) | through Jun12 | (Day 52) = | 52 Days = | Cyclotone 2 = | ORANGE |
| Jun 13 (Day 1) | through Aug 3 | (Day 52) = | 52 Days = | Cyclotone 3 = | YELLOW |
| Aug 4 (Day 1) | through Sep 24 | (Day 52) = | 52 Days = | Cyclotone 4 = | GREEN |
| Sep 25 (Day 1) | through Nov 15 | (Day 52) = | 52 Days = | Cyclotone 5 = | SKY BLUE |
| Nov 16 (Day 1) | through Jan 6 | (Day 52) = | 52 Days = | Cyclotone 6 = | INDIGO |
| Jan 7 (Day 1) | through Feb 28 | (Day 52) = | 52 Days = | Cyclotone 7 = | VIOLET |

Leap Year birthdays are frustrating, because technically speaking, you only have a birthday every four years! But of course, most such people go ahead and celebrate on either February 28 or March 1. However, if you are a true Leap Year baby, remember to calculate your Cyclotones as shown above. And, as with Jan 8 birthdays, February 29 is not included in your count.

Birthdays which fall on January 8 and February 29 signify a positive alignment with a past life. This could indicate a continuity of talent and/or relationships. There are specific karmic ties to someone or something, and it is quite possible that if you express your talent in this life, it will be considered outstanding. If a karmic relationships is reestablished, this will be a special bond.

Free will will determine the success of the talent or relationship: the intensity of the karmic connection can make it either joyous or totally disastrous! As always, it's all up to you. A complete Gnothology Chart would shine much light on such a situation, so if you have either of the WHITE birthdays, I strongly recommend compiling a chart for yourself and your loved ones.


# Normal Birthdays


## MAY 3 BIRTHDAY

| | | | | | | |
|---|---|---|---|---|---|---|
| May 3 (Day 1) | through Jun 23 | (Day 52) = | 52 Days = | Cyclotone 1 = | RED |
| Jun 24 (Day 1) | through Aug 13 | (Day 52) = | 52 Days = | Cyclotone 2 = | ORANGE |
| Aug 14 (Day 1 | through Oct 5 | (Day 52) = | 52 Days = | Cyclotone 3 = | YELLOW |
| Oct 6 (Day 1) | through Nov 26 | (Day 52) = | 52 Days = | Cyclotone 4 = | GREEN |
| Nov 27 (Day 1) | through Jan 18 | (Day 52) = | 52 Days = | Cyclotone 5 = | SKY BLUE |
| Jan 19 (Day 1) | through Mar 11 | (Day 52) = | 52 Days = | Cyclotone 6 = | INDIGO |
| Mar 12 (Day 1) | through May 2 | (Day 52) = | 52 Days = | Cyclotone 7 = | VIOLET |

As you can see, any normal birthday is *included* in calculating the first day of the first Cyclotone. However, when delineating regular birthday Cyclotones, DO NOT INCLUDE EITHER JANUARY 8 OR FEBRUARY 29 IN YOUR COUNT!

## EXAMINING YOUR CYCLOTONES

The above delineations should show you that the seven Cyclotones extend their influences for quite a long time. They color and help determine exactly how you are going to express all that you are.

For example, if a friend refuses you a favor, your conscious mind probably understands his character well enough to know what to expect from him. But the real reason why he refused you is found in the appropriate Cyclotone! The Cyclotone affects your decision-making process from day to day. This accounts for the times when you change your mind about something without understanding why. Knowing your Cyclotones (and those of your friends and relatives) can help you gain a deeper understanding of why you and they do the things you do. Cyclotones are expressed through the personality, and by recognizing their impact you can eliminate much Karmic Stress.

The individual expression of Cyclotones must always be taken into consideration. If, for example, an individual has a tendency to be timid and withdrawn, this person will not absorb the same amount of Cyclotone 1 energy as an outgoing, strong-minded individual might. Only in extreme circumstances would this happen.

Another person, who is exceptionally open and enjoys companionship, is going to be more receptive to Cyclotone 2 than our former example. The strong-minded individual may use his Cyclotone energy as a means of getting his own way. His method of expressing Cyclotone 2 energy might, for example, be the best business deal he's made for the past seven weeks or more.

Every tool of divination adds to the skill of the esoteric scholar. Use the following formula:

1. Learn the Cyclotones well. Understand what they mean and HOW they can be recognized.

2. Learn HOW to apply your knowledge to your present mode of divination (astrology, Gnothology, Tarot, etc.).
3. Learn HOW to look back and critique your observations.
4. Learn HOW you react to your Cyclotones. Examine the patterns of previous Cyclotone energies. Did you use them well?
5. Learn HOW to prepare for the Cyclotone energies and HOW to use them NOW.

Later in this chapter, I will explain the energies and color influences of each of the seven Cyclotones.

## CYCLOTONE CALENDAR

It's a good idea to mark your calendar as you delineate your personal Cyclotones. When making future plans, keep your Cyclotones in mind. Indeed, be very conscious of all your esoteric patterns. Use them whenever possible. Decision-making and mood graphing are conducive to good future results.

Remember that everyone you meet is also governed by the influence of Cyclotones to some degree. If you want to ask for a raise, why not check the boss's birthday? After all, if he tends to be domineering and strong-willed, it is important that you know his Cyclotone. Study the Cyclotone Chart first and look for compatible cycles.

The current Cyclotone identifies the energy that motivates all present cycles. The nature of each Cyclotone offers a different approach. It's like wearing different clothes. You feel a little different and act a little different, but basically you are still the same.

## COLOR AND CYCLOTONES

Each time you expose yourself to your current Cyclotone color the vibratory input of the Cyclotone is increased. Use your current color in many ways: add touches to your decor and clothing; flowers and candles contribute wonderful supportive energies.

Keep in mind that the influence of your Cyclotone affects your general attitude and approach. An aversion to a particular color suggests a resistance to the type of energy associated with that color. If you find this to be true, don't continue to avoid the color. Gradually introduce lighter shades and tones. This can be done with small decor items—a picture frame, candle, cushion, coffee mug. Even a pen or handkerchief kept in your purse or pocket will prove helpful in enabling you to accept the color.

A dislike of a certain color is not unusual. A good example might be an aversion to your Soul Color, found in the Advanced Gnothology Chart.* This particular Aspect on your Natal Chart is vitally important. All Original Level Aspects should be identified and worked on. They represent the rudiments of your Karmic Purpose. Color is the first key, and the acceptance and use of your Soul Color can shift the balance in your favor and provide you with a comfortable feeling of stability and harmony.

## THE INFLUENCES OF CYCLOTONES

### Cyclotone 1 = RED

The best time of the year to take command is governed by Cyclotone 1, which normally includes your birthday as Day 1 of its 52-day cycle. Look at your life as it really is and watch for every opportunity. Take an interest in your appearance. Take care of loose ends. Your personality and talents can now be recognized, so be ready! Project yourself forward; develop more confidence and ability.

Be firm with yourself and evaluate your present circumstances. Examine every facet of your life and polish each of them. Once you have everything in order, you will attract positive situations into your life. Under this influence you can originate many new projects; put some shine on old plans and see them come to life. The force of Cyclotone 1 propels the personal success you desire.

Add a little RED to your clothing or keep a RED handkerchief in a pocket or purse. During this period get back in shape and allow the vitality and radiance of this Cyclotone to work for you.

*See: *The Connolly Book of Numbers, Vol. I*, Chapter 6, p. 33, and *Vol. II*, Chapter 3, pp. 27–28, "Procedure 46: Color Blocking."

## Cyclotone 2 = ORANGE

Relax as the Root Chakra now comes to another focus. You will feel the energy of this Cyclotone urging you to look beyond yourself. Open your eyes and recognize the people around you.

You can give and receive much support. As Cyclotone 2 becomes stabilized, you will feel more compassionate and concerned about others. Your intuition becomes sharpened and you can achieve success through both new and old contacts. Let yourself be open to discussion. Be prepared to listen and you will discover hitherto unknown outlets and avenues of potential success.

Steer away from being impulsive. Think things out before you air your views. Under this Cyclotone influence you will become more aware of people close to you. If you have a partner, your relationship can improve tremendously just by showing more interest in this person. You will be surprised at how you can both rediscover old feelings. The Sacral Chakra is also very responsive to the vibrations of Cyclotone 2. As the energies increase during this period, be alert to a new romance, new and exciting relationships. Women can get pregnant, for this Cyclotone has the esoteric qualities of spring and nature. It is a wonderful time to discover love in all types of relationships. Reunions, trips and solving relationship problems are also possible during this period.

## Cyclotone 3 = YELLOW

As you enter this new Cyclotone cycle, don't expect too much from others. You may want to lean a little on someone and feel terribly hurt if no one offers support. Self-confidence is important, as you have so much you want to do and say. Begin this cycle in a realistic way: STOP and take a good look at your life. Repair, correct and complete all situations that are now preventing you from living the way you desire. Before accepting new projects and new circumstances, be sure to think it all out first.This Cyclotone provides a sweeping new energy, and utmost care must be taken when applying it to your life.

It is an excellent time to start focusing on health and diet. Cyclotone 3 energy provides the stamina needed to maintain discipline in these areas. This same energy can be used to solve old, tired problems. They can be cleared up once and for all! Anticipating this Cyclotone, you should be ready to use its energy immediately. Be willing to let go of old emotional weaknesses. Once this is accomplished, the nature of the Cyclotone can transform you. Your personality becomes more attractive, confidence is implanted and goals become more realistic. Your creativity is awakened. Life presents many choices. You look better and feel better. Clear out old emotional patterns, experiment with new ideas. This can be a time of personal expression and joy.

## Cyclotone 4 = GREEN

Discover the confidence to explore all your needs. Listen to your inner voice and allow your karmic memory to motivate your desires. Under the compelling influence of Cyclotone 4 you can confidently build new, strong foundations. You may have to push to remove the debris of confused desires, but now is the right time to achieve this. Don't be afraid of beginning again. Start new projects if you have the plans clear in your mind. Concentrate and put yourself exactly where you know you should be. Listen to your intuitive level. Avoid being overly influenced by others and stick to your guns.

Regardless of your age, this Cyclotone touches on your deepest desires and frustrations, creating the urge to study and start new projects. It's never too late! Satisfy your inner needs and enjoy new ventures. Rearrange your home, clean out drawers and cupboards, rid yourself of unwanted and unnecessary items. You have an opportunity to start over again. Make new plans, investigate new possibilities and don't be afraid to explore. The power to take control is now yours, but first remove your debris. Do this in the early part of your Cyclotone and then enjoy the challenge and excitement of discovering the new you!

## Cyclotone 5 = SKY BLUE

Every color of BLUE will enhance Cyclotone 5. The ultimate color level of SKY BLUE will solidify as a result of your expansion. Now is the time to reach out and express a sense of inner freedom. Let go of fears and experience the release of the "old you." Discover exciting new outlets of expression. Your aura becomes imbued with the energy of this Cyclotone. During this period be open to new and innovative ideas. Many surprises and changes will occur. Examine, question and act accordingly. Let your natural impulses guide you at this time.

You are likely to be more adventurous. Now is the time to travel, if possible. Many karmic situations are being presented to you. You will want to peel away old, tired concepts like a banana. Contacts with new people and situations can be very useful in the future. Avoid limiting your outlook. Your mind becomes keen and sharp. You will see things in a different light. Act upon this vibrant force and prepare for the unexpected.

Excitement is in the air. Look in many directions and feel new possibilities. Light up your dreams with the many alternatives. Use your mind well, for your intellect is sharpened. Think things out and put your thoughts into action.

## Cyclotone 6 = INDIGO

This is a renewing and revitalizing period. Feel the deep desire to relax and enjoy all your blessings. This is a time for making contact with loved ones again. A letter, a phone call or card will help you release your innermost feelings. Take a good long look at life and allow your love to spread all through it. Reevaluate all that you have. Take the time to let those you love know that you care.

Cyclotone 6 penetrates and activates your deep sense of responsibility. Don't be surprised if you find yourself walking down "memory lane." It is a time for forgiveness and acceptance, a time to forget past hurts and mistakes. You are in the process of firming up your basic roots and foundations. It is from this vibratory level that other Cyclotones receive power for future direction. The future is important; now is the time to establish the seeds.

Proposals, engagements and commitments are given and received. Both personal and business activities are affected on this level. Long-term plans can come to fruition when they are established in this Cyclotone. Use the energy and you will be preparing for new prosperity. It is a fortunate and opportune time for obtaining favors and agreements. Cultivating and improving relationships will be uppermost in your mind. This is very positive energy and can help erase any existing negativity. Your physical appearance will become more important to you. Change your look, experiment with style. Invite friends over. The new you is trying to emerge.

## Cyclotone 7 = VIOLET

Be ready to understand the nature and value of this beautiful Cyclotone 7. As the color tones change from VIOLET to PURPLE, you are constantly reminded of your security and place in life. The depth of this energy removes unnecessary elements; you must avoid resisting its therapeutic workings. How you react to the subtle changes will determine your capacity to accept a new whole Cyclotonal frequency.

It is the time for open-air activities. You can gain this Cyclotonal level just by taking a walk. Your physical body is endeavoring to become attuned to the universal forces. Meditation can reinforce your spiritual development, thus attaining the Cyclotonal desire. This period precedes the beginning of a new cycle of Cyclotone frequencies. Enjoy being alone, and take this time to renew. Your physical body requires this energy period to release all negativity and renew itself. Music can help raise the vibratory level; through this Cyclotone you can replenish each level of consciousness.

New strength is forming and preparing for each new Cyclotone. Allow yourself to enjoy the simple things in life. If possible, avoid involvement in new ventures. Be patient and wait for the next Cyclotone. Give existing affairs your attention and recognize that the energy of this Cyclotone is working to solidify exactly what you need. Allow it to clear away unwanted situations. It is a perfect time to begin your spiritual search. You will feel the need to explore your own true potential. This is a deep and exciting need. Examine it and discover the source of your curiosity. Know that the keys to achieving a Cyclotonal level are tranquility and acceptance.

# CHAPTER 18

# TAROT, THE GATEWAY TO CYCLOTONES

The Major Arcana of the Tarot deck portray a pictorial spiritual journey of the soul. The complete Tarot deck is made up of 78 cards, with 22 of these known as the Major Arcana. These Major cards can be considered a distillation of undiluted wisdom, designed to be used for serious meditation as well as for divination. The remaining 56 cards are known as the Minor Arcana and are used solely for divination.

The Major Arcana are a fascinating and deeply rewarding esoteric study which any student of spiritual knowledge should become familiar with. Starting as an Apprentice, you explore the fundamentals of the Tarot: the mystery of the cards is unveiled, and you learn how to use them for meditation and divination. Your exciting study continues as a Jouneyman, where, now exposed to the ancient wisdom and secrets, you develop your skills and learn the language of Tarot in preparation for becoming a Master. If the study of Tarot interests you, I suggest you consult my two previous volumes on the subject.*

In this book, we will be using seven of the Major Arcana cards as focuses to help you enter the nucleus of each separate Cyclotone, thus attaining the Cyclotonal Level. You do not have to be an expert in Tarot to avail yourself of this wonderful opportunity. In fact, you need no previous experience with the cards at all. I will explain fully the content and meaning of the seven cards we will be using.

The seven Major cards will become a Gateway to enter the center

---

*See: *Tarot: A New Handbook for the Apprentice* (Newcastle, 1979) and *Tarot: The Handbook for the Journeyman* (Newcastle, 1987).

of the Cyclotonal Level. The hidden symbolism in each card instigates the vibratory frequency needed to enter the Gateway and explore the regions of spiritual consciousness. You will experience the unexplainable joy of true self-awareness on the esoteric level of the Cyclotones.

Later on, we will continue our Karmic Meditations, and I will give you a beautiful and powerful meditation for each of the seven cards. Now here are the seven Major Arcana we will work with and their correlation with the Cyclotones:

## CYCLOTONAL CORRELATIONS WITH THE MAJOR ARCANA

| | | | |
|---|---|---|---|
| 1. | THE MAGICIAN | CYCLOTONE 1 | RED |
| 2. | THE HIGH PRIESTESS | CYCLOTONE 2 | ORANGE |
| 3. | THE EMPRESS | CYCLOTONE 3 | YELLOW |
| 4. | THE EMPEROR | CYCLOTONE 4 | GREEN |
| 5. | THE HIEROPHANT | CYCLOTONE 5 | SKY BLUE |
| 6. | THE LOVERS | CYCLOTONE 6 | INDIGO |
| 7. | THE CHARIOT | CYCLOTONE 7 | VIOLET |

## PREPARING FOR THE GATEWAY

Before proceeding further it is important for you to reflect on your personal Cyclotone. Take the time to analyze your present condition. Ask yourself pertinent questions and be sure that the answers are accurate. You must have accurate knowledge of your present status. Be aware of both your misgivings and your potential.

Make no promises to yourself at this time. Assess things exactly as they are. Avoid the urge to make excuses. Be open and you will gain far more when you enter the Gateway. As you contemplate and recognize past and present mistakes, try not to be overly concerned at this point. The whole purpose of entering the Gateway to your Cyclotone is to find out HOW and WHERE you begin.

Studying your Cyclotones will also prove to be helpful. You are now experiencing a different energy level, so you can be objective and see whether you used your last Cyclotone to your advantage. As you recognize missed opportunities and incomplete efforts, you will achieve a better understanding of why you feel as you do at this time. Reflection can often penetrate your consciousness better than reality. So as you prepare for contemplation, examine your achievements and failures. See how you have previously availed yourself of your Cyclotone and see how you caused yourself stress when you didn't.

If your past difficulties involved another person, look at their Cyclotone and see whether the conflict was related to your Cyclotones. If you don't work with the current energy, then you are working against it. Opposing a Cyclotone is like trying to oppose a hurricane. So welcome each change, be ready for the new and necessary energy levels. The universal flow is the source of your personal flow. No matter what life presents, if you are in rhythm with your personal cycles, you can ride with the waves.

Extract the seven Major cards listed above from your Tarot deck and spend some time looking at them. Handle the cards and your vibrations will energize their symbols. You are going to use these cards for specific meditation procedures. Take care of them and become familiar with each individual card. The strength of each card is invaluable. Mere exposure to the Major symbols can alert your Higher Consciousness.

Make sure that the cards you purchase are complementary to your receptivity. You can do this by allowing your basic instincts to work for you. If you immediately like the cards and respond easily to their colors and symbols, then you have discovered your seven Gateways. Protect the seven cards you extract and also the remaining deck. Put them away when they are not in use.

Use the basic meditation procedure. Lighting a candle in your present Cyclotone Color will create a good atmosphere for meditation. Express your Cyclotone Color in any way possible. A piece of ribbon or scarf worn loosely around your neck heightens the meditative process.

Achieving the Cyclotonal Level begins with a deep, true desire to reach the center of your Cyclotone. With serious intent, patience and practice you can elevate your present level of consciousness to the Cyclotonal Level. From this level you are given clear vision and the power to change according to your karmic needs. Entering the Gateway immediately removes Karmic Stress. The wisdom and strength to maintain this level is obtained when you have achieved Cyclotonal Consciousness.

This supreme level elevates your present consciousness to a state of true knowing. You reach complete realization of your own spiritual level. The Greek words, *Gnothe seauton* ("Know thyself") explain the spiritual level we call Cyclotonal. Once this level is obtained, your life improves immediately. Your focus becomes steady and your activities no longer cause stress. Discovering your true purpose eliminates the need to gain satisfaction elsewhere. Each small attainment is recognized as self-achievement. Your soul derives a deep satisfaction as you reach a state of joy and contentment. The absence of Karmic Stress opens a new vista of opportunity. From the center of the Cyclotonal Consciousness the security of knowing provides the physical body with abundant health, and the Path of Destiny becomes a journey of deepest meaning.

# THE SEVEN MAJOR ARCANA

**MAJOR ARCANA: I**
**NAME: THE MAGICIAN**
**CYCLOTONE: 1**
**COLOR: RED**

You see a vibrant young man with one arm stretched up toward the heavens, his other hand glowing in response. Before him is a table and on it are the tools of the Higher Consciousness. Surrounded by the beauty of his spiritual environment, you can almost feel his energies creating exactly what he wants.

He is expressing his true desires, applying effort toward his own cause. You see in his eyes the belief, the knowing, as he creates and extends his life force. His body ripples with inner strength as he exerts himself and reaches up to the True Source. He is determined; he knows that he can produce everything he needs with the tools on his table. Lifting up to his Higher Consciousness, he will manifest all he needs.

THE MAGICIAN

MAJOR ARCANA: II
NAME: THE HIGH PRIESTESS
CYCLOTONE: 2
COLOR: ORANGE

The beautiful High Priestess sits between two majestic pillars. Behind her you see the gates of Daath. Beyond these gates are the true garden and the new dawn of consciousness. Holding the Torah scroll, she invites you to explore the mystical regions of your own being.

Sitting on the threshold of the Higher Consciousness, she offers knowledge and true joy. The Pool of Spirituality at her feet indicates your need to go beyond the GOLDEN gates and discover the true meaning and purpose of your life path. Her beauty and tranquility bring peace to your soul. She is ready and willing to hear your pleas and share your deepest desires.

THE HIGH PRIESTESS

MAJOR ARCANA: III
NAME: THE EMPRESS
CYCLOTONE: 3
COLOR: YELLOW

This regal figure in a vivid PINK gown is sitting in a field of ripe wheat. Abundance surrounds her as she sits at the center of her power. Twelve GOLDEN stars encircled by living leaves form a crown upon her head. The Empress has abundance and power. She represents fulfillment in all human things. The Earth Mother extends her power to all.

To her left is the Fountain of Life. The butterfly is the symbol of rebirth. As the Empress waits for you to enter, she radiates encouragement and understanding. On her breast she wears the GOLDEN symbol of Venus. All that she is, she now offers to you. Her beauty comes from within; all that you see is yours. Know it to be so.

THE EMPRESS

MAJOR ARCANA: IV
NAME: THE EMPEROR
CYCLOTONE: 4
COLOR: GREEN

The Emperor represents discipline, command and authority. His decisions are based on solid foundations. His individuality is firm and he does not allow free expression to govern his need for discipline. Intellect, law and order are the roots of his kingdom.

Control is the key to the Emperor. He is patient and plans well. Ruling with unswaying discipline, he waits. With mind over matter and goals firmly established, he has the greatest vision of all. The PINK-tipped crocus reminds us that spring is arriving. The time is near when you must conserve your strength for the harvest of your success.

THE EMPEROR

MAJOR ARCANA: V
NAME: THE HIEROPHANT
CYCLOTONE: 5
COLOR: SKY BLUE

Wearing the Triple Crown, he is sometimes known as the Pope. He represents external religion and tradition. Traditionally he understands all the ways of man. Before him are two young men. One is still and absorbs what is given. The other listens but knows there is more.

Principles and ideals should always be firmly established. You must also realize that to seek wisdom is to venture beyond. Fear of being yourself makes you a stranger to yourself. In the security of your contentment you must take flight and express every facet of your soul. You must break the barriers of your fears and explore the wisdom that is within the reach of your comprehension.

THE HIEROPHANT

MAJOR ARCANA: VI
NAME: THE LOVERS
CYCLOTONE: 6
COLOR: INDIGO

In the center of this card you see the Tree of Life. It is heavily laden with fruit. All levels of Consciousness are represented here. The man represents the conscious level, which is seeking answers. He looks to the woman, who represents the subconscious level. Her attention is on the cherub, the Higher Consciousness, who conveys the meaning of wisdom and joy.

Overhead you see the great ANGEL RAPHAEL. He is the essence of the universal force. You are shown the man directing his query to the beautiful bird poised on his hand. You are also shown how he can acquire his answers by directing his conscious thoughts through his subconscious and up to the Higher Consciousness. In doing so, he will eat the fruit of the Tree of Life.

THE LOVERS

MAJOR ARCANA: VII
NAME: THE CHARIOT
CYCLOTONE: 7
COLOR: VIOLET

This card shows the warrior riding home after his conquest. He is triumphant and victorious, but his eyes are full of pain as he leaves behind him the aftermath of battle. Holding the reins tightly, he maintains control. His banner of achievement has bright stars, denoting his deeper level of understanding. The Temple of Truth stands firmly behind him.

The warrior has learned to conquer his fears. He has fought many battles. He knows there will be more. Many will still challenge his strength, for the fight for inner freedom is the battle of life. His ability to maintain control never slackens, for he knows that if he is unprepared he cannot conquer.

THE CHARIOT

## PRAYING FOR PERSONAL STRENGTH

The greatest tools of personal strength are prayers. The act of prayer is not only uplifting but also energizing. Prayers are like arrows piercing through the clouds of negativity. But remember that unlike arrows, prayers never fall back to the ground. They always reach their destination. The answers are often waiting on the other side of your despair.

Prayer must be understood. The very act of prayer is a cry for help. It may be a desperate cry, but nevertheless it is always received. You often become so involved and unbalanced in your fear and pain that your expectation is not necessarily the way in which you will receive an answer to your prayer.

Think of this for a moment: Possibly you are distressed, lonely and afraid. You know you are experiencing pain that you cannot handle yourself. You pray to be relieved of your miserable situation. Your solution, your desired answer, is also born in the same misery. This process of prayer is limited because this is what happens:

1. You pray with every atom of your soul.
2. The reason for your misery stems from a dilemma you can't solve.
3. In this state you also formulate the answer, which you cannot know.

This does not make any sense . Here is the correct formula for prayer:

YOU PRAY AND BELIEVE. Even as you pray, you are in the process of receiving your answer.

Daily prayer works like a tonic. Every day you ask for strength and understanding. This means that every day you are receiving strength and understanding. The long, long periods of time between one dramatic life event and another allow you the privilege of mishandling your personal affairs.

Using prayer as a last resort indicates that you have burned many bridges. Isn't it better to pray before you build these bridges? Develop a healthy habit of daily prayer. You will be surprised how much tolerance and patience you acquire. Relax and become familiar with prayer. The Master knows your needs before you do and He knows that you think you know them. Go on automatic spiritual control. Switch off your conscious level and allow the Higher Consciousness to inspire your future actions and decision-making.

Praying is talking to someone you love and who loves you regardless of everything. There is absolutely no need to be embarrassed or to speak eloquently. Just release the pressure and let everything fall away from you. After prayer you should be still for a little while. Be quiet and surround yourself with WHITE light. Wait and feel the new energy being absorbed in every part of you. This new strength will fortify your faith, and you can then go about your daily work and know that everything is going to be fine.

Practice being still and allowing your thoughts to subside. Allow WHITE light to enter every part of your body. Cut yourself off from outside activity and wait. During moments like these you can experience great inspiration. Answers often come into the conscious level. Often they come in the form of new ideas, or maybe you'll receive an impulse to call someone. Answers to prayers are as mysterious as the source from whence they come.

Your prayers are often answered through another human being who unknowingly receives the inspiration to solve your problem. There are many ways to receive answers. Prayers are never ignored. The universal forces begin to manifest and balance immediately as you pray. Have the confidence to look for your answers in every situation you experience. The key to your answer is in your Higher Consciousness. As you are a part of your dilemma, so you become a part of the answer. When you have no apparent need to pray for, then continue your prayer, asking for blessings for all those in need.

CHAPTER 19

# CYCLOTONAL PRAYERS AND MEDITATIONS

In this chapter, I will give you a series of Prayers, Affirmations and Karmic Meditations for the Gateway. There will be four parts to the procedure for each Cyclotone and its corresponding Major Arcanum:

1. Entrance Prayer for the Gateway
2. Cyclotonal Prayer
3. Affirmations
4. Meditation

When used together, these processes are very powerful and will take you through the Gateway and into the Cyclotonal Level.

## ENTRANCE PRAYER FOR THE GATEWAY

1. Hold the card that corresponds to your Cyclotone before you. Look carefully at every detail. Imagine movement in what you see: feel the breeze, smell the flowers and see them dancing in the wind, touch the fabrics of garments.

2. Bring the card to your Inner Eye for a few seconds. Transfer the picture to the center of your chakra.

3. Keeping this picture in your Inner Eye, bring the card down to your Umbilical Chakra. Allow the feelings of the card and the movements in the picture to flow into your body.

4. Now repeat your Cyclotonal Prayer.

5. When you finish, relax and enter the Meditation that corresponds to your Cyclotone.

# CYCLOTONAL PRAYER 1

## THE MAGICIAN/Cyclotone 1 (RED)

I pray for strength to do all the things I must do. I feel the weight of responsibility and I am not sure where to begin. My needs weigh heavily and I find it hard to feel confident. Open my mind so that I may be aware and sensitive to all that happens today. Give me the grace to listen to others, to feel the needs and concerns of all those around me. Let my thoughts and intentions be good and clear. Before I commit myself to obligations, let me first be sure that I can fulfill my promise. My sensitivity is easily touched. When this happens I feel afraid and my strength drains away. I am full of pride and need constant recognition. I know this is a weakness that prevents me from reaching the success I want. Be with me this day and this night. Take away my fear and let me feel the strength and power of your presence. Amen.

Now take a few minutes to feel the Presence. . . .

Now make your Affirmations to . . . THE MAGICIAN.

# AFFIRMATIONS 1

1. I feel the strength and power within me.
2. I am now allowing the universal energies to flow into me.
3. I can feel my inner strength rising.
4. I have purpose and will achieve this purpose.
5. I am capable of many things; I will take control.
6. I feel this control and am truly blessed.
7. I AM THEE I AM. I AM THEE I AM. I AM THEE I AM.

# MEDITATION 15: CYCLOTONE 1/THE MAGICIAN

These four procedures, then, are the proper modus operandi to release you instantly from any possible overlap of the preceding Cyclotone effects. The Prayer and Affirmations may be used daily, and the Meditation can be done when you have sufficient time to relax and enjoy the process.

After the basic meditation preparation, you are now relaxed and feeling very comfortable. Use the proper color (RED) in every way you can. A RED candle and fresh flowers (roses, camellias) will increase the vibratory atmosphere. Have your MAGICIAN card near your candle and flowers. Anticipate the beauty and change you are going to experience. Allow yourself sufficient time to relax and enjoy the changing of your personal Cyclotone.

Look forward to the Cyclotonal effect when you reach the point of release. As the WHITE light floods your new level of consciousness, all fear and apprehension leaves. You have found your control. You will experience the surge of the new vibratory level and your consciousness will become Cyclotonal.

1. Be still and become aware of the surrounding energies. Feel how they encircle your body in a spiral. See the spiral moving up and down around you. Feel the uneven pattern of intermingling colors.
   Wait. . . .

2. Think of a flower. . . . Now project that flower into the spiral of energies. Watch how quickly the thought of the flower comes back to you. Do this again.
   Wait. . . .

3. Feel how the surrounding vibrations appear to hold you tightly within the spiral.
   Wait. . . .

4. The spiral of energy is a resisting force that you have built around yourself. Within your new Cyclotone you will need clearance so that you can do the things you have to do. Now focus on your CROWN Chakra. Feel your eyes look up to the top center of your head.
   Wait. . . .

5. Breathe in slowly and easily from the SPHERE beneath your feeet. Bring your breath up to your Crown Chakra. Hold it here for the count of THREE and then release it easily and slowly, out of your INNER EYE. Repeat this: Breathe in from the Sphere beneath your feet. Slowly bring your breath up into your Crown Chakra. Hold the breath for a count of three. Exhale slowly and easily through the Inner Eye. Continue to breathe in this manner and feel your Crown Chakra responding and opening.
Wait. . . .

6. Now breathe normally and become aware of the WHITE light above your head. Feel the brilliance and beauty of the universal energies touching your Crown chakra.
Wait. . . .

7. Reaching up through the top of your head, inhale the WHITE light and bring it down to the Sphere beneath your feet. Release the WHITE light through the UMBILICAL Chakra and see the rays coming from the center of your body breaking up the spiral pattern of energy that surrounds you. Repeat the breathing pattern: Reach up through the top of your head and inhale WHITE light. Bring it down to the Sphere beneath your feet. Release the WHITE light through your Umbilical Chakra and allow the outgoing light rays to clear the confining spiral energies. Continue to breathe this way until you see a RED cloud of energy building before you.
Wait. . . .

8. Now feel the glow of RED on your face and body. Let the warm glow of RED flow into every pore. Fill your whole body with the vibrancy of RED energy.
Wait. . . .

9. Now go toward the RED cloud and feel your inner energy building as you wait for your MASTER.
Wait. . . .

10. As your Master appears, you feel the power of his presence. Say:
        I CALL UPON MY MASTER.
        I COME FOR STRENGTH AND KNOWLEDGE.

I ASK FOR GUIDANCE ON MY LIFE PATH.
I AM READY TO RENEW MY SOUL.
Repeat the above four statements.
Now see the RED cloud open. Walk to the center of the cloud and feel its vibratory power energize every part of your being. Wait. . . .

11. You are now ready to see the negative path you are leaving behind. As the cloud opens, feel your inner strength rise. Observe your past attitudes.
Wait. . . .

12. Observe your past weaknesses.
Wait. . . .

13. Observe your past failures.
Wait. . . .

14. Observe your past mistakes.
Wait. . . .

15. Observe your past fears.
Wait. . . .

16. As the cloud enfolds you, you leave all these things behind. Now see LIGHT wrapping around you. Feel that the past is far away. Feel your new protection. Experience the peace and beauty of reaching the Cyclotonal Level.
Wait. . . .

17. Look up above you and see the light. Look before you and see your Master.
Wait. . . .

18. Take your time and tell your Master all the things you must do to put your life in order.
Wait. . . .

19. Before you, the cloud now opens. Step outside and see your immediate future. See the new situations you will create with your new strength. Look at your relationships, look at your life.
Wait. . . .

20. Your Master now leads you to your Inner Temple. As you walk inside, the candle on the altar is burning brightly. The

Inner Temple is peaceful and the Book of Wisdom is open to
you. Read the Karmic Wisdom on its pages.
Wait. . . .

21. Now walk out of your Inner Temple. You are wearing the
Cyclotonal robe of RED. You are now ready for life. You are
blessed with spiritual strength. Give thanks.

Say the following aloud:
I AM NOW IN THE UNIVERSAL LIGHT.
MY MASTER AND THE ANGELS BRING ME STRENGTH
FROM GOD.
I WILL CALL UPON THEM WHEN MY SOUL IS IN NEED.
I AM THEE I AM. I AM THEE I AM. I AM THEE I AM.

Each day renew your Cyclotonal Level with Prayer and Affirmations.

# CYCLOTONAL PRAYER 2

## THE HIGH PRIESTESS/Cyclotone 2 (ORANGE)

Open my heart and mind. Give me the strength to shift the concern I have for myself to others more in need. Shed light on all my dark
corners so that I can face the problems that confront me. Give me the
power to understand the direction of my life. Help me to repair any hurt
I have done to others. My deepest needs are disguised by my unthink-
ing actions. Grant me the ability to see who I really am. Release me from
all my fears. I am often afraid; my soul cries out and in my anxiety I
make unwise decisions and speak unkindly. I come to you now as a lost
child. I long for peace and contentment. I know I am an integral part
of the universal plan. I am ready to find my place. Be with me in every
thought, word and deed. Let me be gentle yet firm in my cause. Let my
heart and words reflect my prayer.

Take a few moments to feel the Presence. . . .

Now make your Affirmations to . . . THE HIGH PRIESTESS.

## AFFIRMATIONS 2

1. I feel the light growing bright within me.
2. I am allowing the light to penetrate my darkness.
3. I can feel the power of a new direction.
4. I have the ability to see the things I must do.
5. I will do these things in love and pure light.
6. I know my past is behind me and I must go forward.
7. I AM THEE I AM. I AM THEE I AM. I AM THEE I AM.

## MEDITATION 16: Cyclotone 2/THE HIGH PRIESTESS

1. Relax and become aware of your SACRAL Chakra filling with intense ORANGE vibrations.
   Wait. . . .

2. Feel the support and strength as the energy restricts itself entirely to your Sacral region.
   Wait. . . .

3. The ORANGE energies now form a magnificent belt of strength around your physical body. As the ORANGE fibers firmly join together, you feel their strength within you and the power of the belt now gripping your physical body.
   Wait. . . .

4. You have been waiting on the edge of the sunset. You are alone; the dying light of the sky is reflected in the ocean before you.
   Wait. . . .

5. Feel the indescribable strength of the ORANGE belt supporting everything that you are. See the glow of the setting sun and let your hands touch the brilliant Buckle of Force that now holds your ORANGE belt.
   Wait. . . .

6. New vitality springs up into your HEART Chakra. You feel a force from the belt begin to form a glow all through your body.
   Wait. . . .

7. As you focus on the setting sun, you are a reflection of everything you see. The sun is slowly going down; now darkness begins to surround you. . . . The only light is the glow around your body. . . . Now focus directly on the ORANGE sun and feel everything that you are begin to drop away slowly. Feel the weight of your body and the flaming desire within to follow the journey of the sun. . . . Now merge with the ORANGE sphere. Completely become one with the sunset. . . . Look back at the ocean, the seashore and the lights in the distance. Wait. . . .

8. Totally relax and feel the energies pulling you down. As you look out before you, watch the colors of the sky change as your light begins to pull you away. Listen to the many prayers that now come from the darkness before you. Absorb these prayers and give them power.
Wait. . . .

9. Everything you are is now being reinforced. The power coming from your Sacral belt is now increasing. You know that you have the personal power to understand your deepest needs. As you feel the pull of this power, allow all negativity, seen and unseen, known and unknown, to fall away. Everything that has prevented your joy is now swiftly leaving. The power of the ORANGE expels the remaining fragments of negativity. They appear to disintegrate like black specks in the magnificent force of your new power.
Wait. . . .

10. As the last remaining influence of negativity completely vanishes, you are free, totally free from any hindrance. You are free to be you. Allow this freedom to flow throughout your body. Start at your feet and feel WHITE light travel slowly up your body and out the top of your head. Hold this new freedom and feel light in every part of your body.
Wait. . . .

11. Standing in light with your Sacral belt of ORANGE, feel the warmth and splendor of the rising sun behind you.
Wait. . . .

12. From the soles of your feet feel the urge of the lifting force of the universe and experience the spiritual joy of being uplifted.
Wait. . . .

13. As you move up with the universal force, become the center of the rising sun behind you. Let yourself become one and see the rays extending from your center.
Wait. . . .

14. You are anxious to give what you have received. You can feel yourself wrenching out of the darkness. You are reaching the horizon of new possibilities. Once again you see the ocean stretched out before you. Your Cyclotonal level of consciousness is now dawning and you can see the light rays of your intentions reflected on the ocean before you.
Wait. . . .

15. Extend a glorious blessing to all those beyond the shore. Let your new spirituality bring hope and joy to all. Reach out in light and touch everything you see, eliminating pain and distress. You *are* the light, you can give your light to this new day.
Wait. . . .

16. You are a part of this new sunrise. With the power of your Sacral belt now push forward into light. Let your feet feel the wet sand. As you walk on the shore, your feet leave new footprints. They glimmer in your light. You are in control; each step will take you away from all Karmic Stress.
Wait. . . .

17. See your MASTER before you. You are greeted warmly with open arms and gentle smile. Ask for his wisdom and share your new decisions with him.
Wait. . . .

18. Look at the horizon and know that you have renewed your personal power. As you see the morning sun rise majestically, feel the power within you rise also. You can now do the things you must do. This day you will use this power. Say farewell to your Master and listen to his parting words of wisdom.
Wait. . . .

19. You are now standing on the shores of your own life. See your reflection in the rising sun.
    Wait. . . .

20. With every part of your being . . . give thanks.

Say the following aloud:
I AM NOW COMPLETELY REPLENISHED.
I AM READY TO LIVE MY LIFE WITHOUT STRESS.
I AM A PART OF EVERY NEW DAY.
I AM THEE I AM. I AM THEE I AM. I AM THEE I AM.

Each day renew your Cyclotonal Level with Prayer and Affirmations.

# CYCLOTONAL PRAYER 3

## THE EMPRESS/Cyclotone 3 (YELLOW)

Thank you for the many blessings of love and life. Each new day fills my heart and soul with fresh hope. Let me come closer to the joyful center of your everlasting love. Give me the strength to acknowledge openly the constant flow of love and concern I receive from others. Broaden my outlook so that I may embrace all the abundance you give me. May all those I meet today share the light I feel in my soul. I am ever grateful to be me. I know I have much to do and you are always with me. Help me to reach beyond my doubts. Awaken my abilities so that I can satisfy my longings. I pray that the fruits of my labor may be shared abundantly with all those I love. Help me to plan objectively. Help me to focus and give nothing but my best. In your divine strength I know that all these things are possible.

Take a few moments to feel the Presence. . . .

Now make your Affirmations to . . . THE EMPRESS.

# AFFIRMATIONS 3

1. I feel the abundance of all my blessings.
2. I am directing myself to joy and love.

3. I can see the light that will support me.
4. I will do all the things I must do and not turn back.
5. I know the strength I need is now manifesting.
6. I see the light, I am the light, I share the light.
7. I AM THEE I AM. I AM THEE I AM. I AM THEE I AM.

## MEDITATION 17: CYCLOTONE 3/THE EMPRESS

1. Feel the blue sky high above your head. You are lying beneath your Tree of Wisdom. Relax and listen to the birds. Listen to all the sounds of nature in your garden.
Wait. . . .

2. This is your garden and you can discover many beautiful things in it. Stand up and look around you. See all the brightly colored flowers. It is a perfect day. The sun is warm and you have a reason to be here. There are many small paths for you to walk. Look for the Path of Relationships. Other paths will attract you, but look for this special path and wait for me there.
Wait. . . .

3. This path, like all paths, will take you to a specific area of your life. This is your garden. All that you see is what you have planted. Now walk along the Path of Relationships. You will find a bench; sit and observe your life's work. First, extend your vision to the early plantings. Each relationship that has influenced you exists in this part of the garden. Examine each one in turn and acknowledge your feelings for these old flowers. Understand how they have affected the pattern of growth throughout your garden.
Wait. . . .

4. Now is the time to do some gardening. First you must remove weeds and dead plants. The ground is hard and thirsty. The old, unwanted growth must be removed so that you can give nourishment to the precious flowers you have neglected. Do this now and do it well. Make sure that you dig deeply and remove the snarled roots of still-thriving but unwanted growth. This must be done now to remove all Karmic Stress.
Wait. . . .

5. Observe your work. Have you uprooted all the years of unwanted growth? You have the time. Take a second look and be sure you have cleared everything.
Wait. . . .

6. Now you see before you the precious flowers that remain. Because of neglect they are in great need of nourishment. Recognize each plant and give it the attention it needs. As you do this, you will see the energy immediately respond: the flowers will become brilliant in color. Openly acknowledge their existence. Your MASTER will work with you, giving advice and direction for the total nourishment of each remaining flower. Listen carefully as you both work together.
Wait. . . .

7. Now look at your work. Your thoughts and intentions have instilled new life on your Path of Relationships. Your Master now leads you to the Fountain of Spirituality. It is a wonderful sight. Go now and bathe. Wash all your regrets away. Feel refreshed as you splash like a child in your new spirituality.
Wait. . . .

8. Now you are ready to explore another path. Look for the Path of Self-Expression. Enjoy the beauty of your garden as you look for the Path of Self-Expression.
Wait. . . .

9. As you walk along this path, you will see a fence surrounding your Garden of Self-Expression. Walk all around this fence. Is it small or large? As you walk around it, look at your plantings. Weeds have grown here and there. Some of these undesirable weeds now completely cover your original concepts. Unlock the gate that surrounds your Garden of Self-Expression and once more do the things you have to do. Be careful that you don't destroy a flower, as it may be hidden away from the light. Be sure that you recognize all the flowers. Recognize what has prevented their growth and remove the weeds accordingly.
Wait. . . .

10. Once again your Master comes to help you. Slowly but surely you begin to recognize all that has happened. Rearrange your plantings as you need them to be. Break down the old fence

that has stifled growth. Work hard and well, for you will gain much power and satisfaction from your efforts.
Wait. . . .

11. As you look at your work, you know that there is no need for a new fence. You must come back often to keep everything in trim. Now wash the pain of labor away. Go once again to the Fountain of Spirituality and enjoy yourself.
Wait. . . .

12. Over to the LEFT you see a cluster of trees. Walk over there; as you leave the warmth of your garden, you feel a change of temperature when you enter your Forest of Desires. It smells wonderful here. Fresh and clean. You will have to look carefully for the tiny flowers of expectation. They are hidden in the tall, green grasses. It is difficult to see where they are. You wonder why they are so spread apart. This is because they were planted in the dark. You were afraid to expose your seeds of belief. In dreams, in tears and desperation, you have run to this beautiful glade to hide your true feelings. Now you feel like a child. Go and pick a posy of expressions that have never been exposed to the warmth and sunlight in your garden. Your Master is with you and will help you to remember what you planted and where.
Wait. . . .

13. Now find your way back to the garden. As you come out of the trees, immediately feel the warmth of new possibilities shining on your face. Find a place by your Fountain of Spirituality and look at what you have picked from your Forest of Desires. Try to understand why you hid these lovely flowers. Go now and wander around your Garden of Abundance and plant these flowers where they should be.
Wait. . . .

14. Your last path is the Path of Inner Peace. This path is now to your immediate RIGHT. Go ahead and enjoy your Garden of Peace. It is always beautiful here. Everything you have accomplished is now a gorgeous flower. See how much beauty there is. Inhale the deep fragrance of contentment. Feel the joy of Inner Peace. Your Master now gives you an exquisite flower.

Ask where you should plant it; then go and discover that part of your garden and plant it carefully and with love.
Wait. . . .

15. As you finish your planting, your Master now gives you another bloom. This is one that you must give to someone else. Ask what it is and whom you must give it to.
Wait. . . .

16. After working in your garden, you are now free to sit like the EMPRESS in the midst of your abundance. Find the center of your garden and you will see your throne waiting.
Wait. . . .

17. Now sit on the splendid Throne of Accomplishment. Sitting here at the center of your garden you can see every part of it. Feel the pleasure of all that is growing. Feel the beauty and abundance of your spiritual garden.
Wait. . . .

18. Feel the power of the sun overhead. Feel the majesty of the EMPRESS and give thanks.

Say the following aloud:
I AM THE CENTER OF ALL THAT I AM.
I AM THE SEASONS OF MY OWN GROWTH.
I REMOVE ALL THE SOURCES OF KARMIC STRESS.
I AM THEE I AM. I AM THEE I AM. I AM THEE I AM.

Each day renew your Cyclotonal Level with Prayer and Affirmations.

# CYCLOTONAL PRAYER 4

## THE EMPEROR/Cyclotone 4 (GREEN)

This day I offer to you. Be with me in all I do and say. Fortify my strength and let me know the meaning of true accomplishment. Give me your love and comfort when I experience weakness. Take away my fears and allow me to recognize the authority and rights of others. Let me feel true respect and have no envy. May I fill this day with good, honest work. Inspire my thoughts, guide my actions and show me the way if I lose myself. Fill me with confidence that is disciplines in light. As I concentrate on the things I must do, let me not forget the feelings of those around me. Let me be considerate and open to those who offer assistance. I want to be receptive to the ideas of others. I want to feel the calmness of my own discipline. Enter my heart with divine light and let every effort come only from this light.

Take a few moments to feel the Presence. . . .

Now make your Affirmations to . . . THE EMPEROR.

## AFFIRMATIONS 4

1. I feel my anxiety and fears leaving me.
2. I will be true to myself; my strength is the light.
3. I now take control of my life and will reach my goals.
4. I have the Inner Light to support my new confidence.
5. I am open and receptive, with new courage in my soul.
6. I feel a new inspiration to accomplish and succeed.
7. I AM THEE I AM. I AM THEE I AM. I AM THEE I AM.

## MEDITATION 18: CYCLOTONE 4/THE EMPEROR

1. As you relax, go back to your earliest conscious memories. Try to focus on the first blocks, the early memories of your first efforts. Look at your early disappointments. Without any emotion try to understand what caused these blockages. Was it a lack of sufficient effort? Did you rely on someone else? Or was it just a simple case of not being able to cope? Review these early patterns and try to see exactly what caused your blockages.
Wait. . . .

2. Now bring your thoughts forward to recent years. Consider again the reasons why you have not achieved your goals in certain areas.
Wait. . . .

3. Look beneath the surface and decide whether the basic reasons for your lack of achievement are identical to those of your early years. Are you still using the same old thought patterns? Does your memory find a convenient file that explains all your failures? There is a file named Discipline. This is a large file, with sub-headings: Family. Relationships. School. Work. Money. Health. Love. These are just a few.

   Once you delegate authority to any of the sub-files, you are giving away your right to discipline your life. Karmic Stress occurs when this right is relinquished through fear of careless-ness. Your personal direction must be a result of your com-mand. Consider who is holding your power. Who have you given it to, knowingly or unknowingly?
   Wait. . . .

4. You will now find your lost disciplines. See yourself standing in a beautiful green field. Before you is a mountain. The top of the mountain is hidden in clouds. You feel good as you look at this mountain. This is your mountain, and the peak, which is now covered in clouds, represents your success.
   Wait. . . .

5. As you look at your mountain, you can see many paths that you have climbed. Lifting your vision higher, you can see the sheer, straight rocks. Each time you climb to this level you are confronted with these seemingly impassable rocks. Sometimes you have fallen in your efforts. Other times you have returned to the field below. The reason for past failures is lack of preparation.

   Behind you is your Karmic Tool Shed. Your Original Plan and tools are all there, but you have no key to get inside. Your key is personal discipline. You will find this precious key by looking closely into the last situation where you gave it away! Look for this situation and see how you gave away your key.
   Wait. . . .

6. Your personal key of discipline has been passed around. It is now time to retrieve this key. Examine the situation and deter-mine what you must do to regain it. Without it, you have no

access to your Karmic Tool Shed. What must you do to get your key? Formulate a disciplined plan.
Wait. . . .

7.  Standing beside you is your MASTER. You have made decisions and decided how to retrieve your personal key of discipline. Ask your Master whether your thoughts are correct. Listen to his wisdom.
Wait. . . .

8.  When you fully understand the situation and realize the things you must do, then your Master will give you the key.
Wait. . . .

9.  Now go to your Karmic Tool Shed. Your Master accompanies you. Unlock the door and close it behind you. It is rather dark inside. Wait until the light around you brightens and you can see the table and chair in the center of the shed.
Wait. . . .

10. Sit at the table; you will see a dusty file box with your name on it. Look inside and see how your Original Plan has been prepared. Beginning with your birth, you have a file for each year. In each of these files are your relationships and all that you have done. Ask your Master which file you must now open.
Wait. . . .

11. Take out the file your Master indicates and spread it open before you on the table. Your Master now offers you a goblet. It is the nectar of life. It is discipline. Drink it now. Feel the strength of discipline surging through your body. You are no longer apprehensive; you feel the power of your own command.
Wait. . . .

12. You now have the appropriate information before you. Note the year; is it an old file or is it current? Look at what area of your life is being affected by your lack of discipline.
Wait. . . .

13. Ask your Master how you can remove the blockages you have seen. Discover your weaknesses and see the type of discipline

that must be used. Contemplate how you will implement this discipline. Allow your Master to help you.
Wait. . . .

14. You now have the plan. You are anxious to establish your discipline. Leave the Karmic Tool Shed and close the door behind you. Give the key of personal discipline to your Master. It will always be there for you to use. Now look at your mountain. The clouds have gone and you can see the first Peak of Success.
Wait. . . .

15. As you walk across the field toward the mountain, keep your mind focused on your new discipline. You are now ready to climb. You know the path you must take. Begin your climb and stick to your Original Plan. You may encounter difficulty, but remember you are now on the right path. You will see alternate paths that look much easier, but remember, they come to a dead end. Stay on your path. You may feel that you can allow yourself more time. Ignore this temptation, or you will find yourself in the darkness of your own dilemma. Concentrate on the things you must do and climb the sheer rock. Your Master is in front of you; keep your focus on his light.
Wait. . . .

16. Don't allow your thoughts to stray. Be determined to stay on this path. It is the *only* path that will take you to the Peak of Success. Look up now and you will see the serenity of the peak. It is unbelievably beautiful. The EMPEROR sits there calmly, waiting for your final effort. Reach out with your fingers for the grassy mound above the sharp Rock of Resistance. Feel yourself being lifted in mind, body and soul. Now stand at the top of your mountain. Look at the pink-tipped crocus heralding a new spring in your life. The EMPEROR now steps off his throne and, smiling in approval, beckons you to take your rightful place. Sit on your throne and look at the fresh new wonders of life that surround you. This is your place of honor. You will come here each time you follow your Original Plan. There is absolutely no Karmic Stress when you have elevated yourself to the throne of the EMPEROR. Enjoy this level of

achievement. Consider what other tools you need to come back here again and again.

Wait. . . .

17. Feel the Crown of Discipline and look as far as the eye can see. You are surrounded by your own world of success. Breathe in the invigorating vibrations. Feel yourself now being brought gently back down to your sunny Field of Decisions. Once more look up and see your place at the Peak of Success. Give thanks for this wonderful experience.

Say the following aloud:

I WEAR THE CROWN OF DISCIPLINE.
I WILL BATTLE TO RETAIN MY CROWN.
I AM FREE TO SIT AT THE PEAK OF MY SUCCESS.
I AM THEE I AM. I AM THEE I AM. I AM THEE I AM.

Each day renew your Cyclotonal Level with Prayer and Affirmations.

## CYCLOTONAL PRAYER 5

## THE HIEROPHANT/Cyclotone 5 (SKY BLUE)

Today I feel the urge to let the light within me expand and comfort others. Before this day ends, may I experience true spiritual joy and before I sleep feel total peace, as I offer you the things I have done. Too long have I been self-centered. Too long have I deprived myself. I have not listened with care to loved ones. I have been too busy with my own concerns. I have cut myself off from the very source of life. My ego has restricted my views and prevented me from knowing who I really am. In my fear and self-protection I have become separated from truth. Beneath my pride and behind my words is the real me. Before I start my day, saturate my soul with divine love so that I can step forward and be a light to all those in the dark.

Take a few moments to feel the Presence. . . .

Now make your Affirmations to . . . THE HIEROPHANT.

## AFFIRMATIONS 5

1. I feel warmth and beauty deep within my soul.
2. I am releasing all barriers; I feel true freedom.
3. I will be considerate to others and envy no one.
4. I can find inner peace today, for I am losing my fear.
5. I have been closed and insensitive but I now open in light.
6. I will discover myself in new thoughts and actions.
7. I AM THEE I AM. I AM THEE I AM. I AM THEE I AM.

## MEDITATION 19:  CYCLOTONE 5/THE HIEROPHANT

1. Let your physical body totally relax. Feel conscious of your weight. Sense the heaviness all around you. You now feel a deep, restricting security. You are secure, yet you are limited. It is an unusual feeling. There is an invisible force; touch it, and as you derive comfort from it, you also experience obstruction. Wait. . . .

2. You are waking from a deep sleep. The four-poster bed is huge, with an ornate canopy. As you look around this large room, you find it very soothing. Your garment is WHITE and you are alone. There is a bell on the bedside table. Ring this bell THREE times and your MASTER will come into the room. Wait. . . .

3. Walk over to the window and see that you are very high up in a turret of your castle. The landscape stretches for miles like a magnificent carpet. You need to dress. Go to the large armoire; you will find clothing in SKY BLUE and also BROWN. You reach for the familiar BROWN and feel good as you dress. Wait. . . .

4. You are now eager to explore your castle. It feels secure and you have wonderful views from the windows. As you descend the stairs, you see the dining room. Standing in the doorway, you observe the exquisite furnishings. On the table there is every kind of food you could desire. There is a fire burning in

the hearth. People are waiting for you. You feel inadequate, ill-dressed for this occasion.

Wait. . . .

5. Your name is repeated over and over again. You know the people are waiting. You make an effort to speak—you can hear your own voice—but they do not hear you. You try to walk through the open door, but you are held back by an invisible force. You can't understand, so you listen to hear what they are saying.

Wait. . . .

6. They can't see you or hear you. You want to leave, so you go to the massive castle doors. It is impossible to open them. You run to a beautiful window in the hall and look out and see sunshine and freedom. You find another door. It too will not open. The castle is lovely; you are not afraid; just bewildered. You see the library. Your Master is at the door. He invites you to sit with him and asks you to look at your clothing. You must dress correctly. Your SKY BLUE clothing is in your room up-stairs. The Master asks you to go back to your room and change your clothing. Do this and then wait for him to knock on your bedroom door.

Wait. . . .

7. You are now dressed in SKY BLUE. You look radiant. Sitting at the fireplace, you feel the warm glow of the flames. You look out the window as you wait for your Master to come.

Wait. . . .

8. When you hear him knock, invite him in. Your Master tells you that you are a prisoner of your self. You spend each day look-ing through the windows of your soul upon landscapes of new opportunity. You constantly fill your castle with exciting guests and prepare feasts to celebrate, but the invisible force which is your fear prevents you from making it all a reality. Instead, you choose the comfort of old BROWN clothes. You lock all your doors, for you are afraid of leaving the security of your castle. Your Master smiles as you realize that you are the source of your own dilemma. Now he leaves you, to wait for you downstairs in the dining room.

You must now open the windows in your room and allow

the Breeze of Desire to come in. It is a wonderful feeling. You can smell the fragrance of roses. Each breath you take is full of new inspiration. Your body, mind and soul are being released.
Wait. . . .

9. You are now anxious to go down the stairway. Open the massive front doors to the castle. Inhale the fragrance of all the flowers growing outside. Run out into the sunshine. Walk around your castle. You will see people here and there smiling as you walk by. Souls from the past and new friends are now waiting in your castle. Enjoy exploring the grounds.
Wait. . . .

10. You are free, perfectly free. As you look at the stone walls of your castle, you see each window open wide. People wave to you. Now they see you, they hear you. You never realized that so many wonderful souls lived in your castle. Smell the fragrance of the rose garden. Enter the garden. Know that the fragrance rises and floats into every window in your castle. You want to take a bouquet of roses back with you, but there are many thorns and you hesitate. Again you can feel the invisible force.
Wait. . . .

11. Your Master is sitting on a bench. Go over to him and he will explain how this garden is the center of all your desires. He will explain that your fear of picking these roses is what causes your conscious mind to lack the Fragrance of Opportunity. You are now given a beautiful rose. Inhale its fragrance and listen to the wisdom of your Master.
Wait. . . .

12. Now you are ready to go back in your castle. As you reach the massive doors, they open wide and you step inside. You realize that you have never opened your castle before. There are many rooms for you to explore. You are free to be who you are. Your Master directs you to a room next to your bedroom. It is the Room of Karmic Talents. In this room are the many things you have accomplished in your past lives. You are anxious to go in. Enter and see clearly all that you have brought with you.
Wait. . . .

13. It is now time to go into the Room of New Possibilities. Your Master beckons and you now enter the next room. Take the vivid memory of your karmic talents with you into the Room of New Possibilities.
Wait. . . .

14. The pulse of life and joy touches every aspect of your soul. Around your neck is a sparkling SKY BLUE jewel. This is your spiritual gift. It is your talent and new opportunity. It sparkles with fresh vitality. You must now go back to your bedroom. Someone very special is waiting for you there. It is someone from your past who has something to say to you.
Wait. . . .

15. After hearing what this person has to tell you, it is time to go to the dining room. This is your celebration, your feast. Go downstairs and take your place at the table.
Wait. . . .

16. Look carefully at the guests sitting at your table. One of them now speaks. Listen and remember what is said.
Wait. . . .

17. You are now free, completely free to express all that you are. You are brimming with new joy and expectation. Give thanks.

Say the following aloud:
I HAVE MY OWN SPECIAL WAYS OF EXPRESSION.
I AM NOT AFRAID TO BE ME.
I HAVE THINGS TO DO AND LOVE TO KNOW.
I AM THEE I AM. I AM THEE I AM. I AM THEE I AM.

Each day renew your Cyclotonal Level with Prayer and Affirmations.


# CYCLOTONAL PRAYER 6

## THE LOVERS/Cyclotone 6 (INDIGO)

I crave peace and tranquility. Every part of my being cries out for the comfort of perfect harmony. So often I make mistakes. I try to please, struggle with my conscience and try to justify my actions. I am often in the dark; I yearn for the light to come into my soul. I have relied on myself and on others, but I am now ready to place this trust in you. I need to think constructively. I need to change many things in my life. I want to come back to my God. As I begin my journey home, I will follow the light. Whatever enters my life from now on will be discarded if it takes me away from the light. Tranquility is now entering my life with the new choices I am making. I will not disturb this inner balance. I will be strong and channel my choices through the divine light.

Take a few moments to feel the Presence. . . .

Now make your Affirmations to . . . THE LOVERS.

# AFFIRMATIONS 6

1. I will reach out today and find peace and harmony.
2. I place my trust and confidence in my God.
3. I can make new choices and find tranquility.
4. I no longer resist the light; it is now in my life.
5. I place my trust in you and I am no longer afraid.
6. I am allowing love and light to balance my thoughts.
7. I AM THEE I AM. I AM THEE I AM. I AM THEE I AM.

# MEDITATION 20: CYCLOTONE 6/THE LOVERS

1. A deep longing for perfect harmony is now filling your body. It fills your mind. Your soul reaches out into the universe, longing for peace, tranquility, balance and harmony. Peace, tranquility, balance and harmony.
   Wait.. . . .

2. Everyday responsibilities press down upon you. It is so easy to sink deeply into your problems. You must let go, you must reach out and leave all this behind. Look before you, look beyond your daily life. See yourself in the distance smiling back. You are standing in WHITE light.
   Wait. . . .

3. Feel the urge to be this other you. Rush forward, leaving all your conscious worries behind. Merge with the WHITE light and absorb the new vibratory level. Instantly you feel the power that is now yours. Look back and see your body comfortable, resting and waiting for the harmony you will bring back.
Wait. . . .

4. Raising your head, you see the splendor of INDIGO. All shades and hues of this color are dancing and pulsating, creating a transcendant harmony. You can hear sounds and you want to see beyond this superb level of beauty.
Wait. . . .

5. In your HEART Chakra you feel a slow, powerful opening, a great sense of release, as you feel a WHITE line of energy now rising to your INNER EYE. It moves slowly. It exhibits a vibrant power as it rises to the Inner Eye.
Wait. . . .

6. Concentrating only on the rising energy, your Inner Eye begins to respond. Eager for the union, you wait till the energy actually touches the Inner Eye. As the merging begins, you feel the Inner Eye Chakra open.
Wait. . . .

7. As the fusing continues, it becomes a brilliant SILVER STAR on your forehead. All that you are is now a part of this star. Feel yourself being lifted up, up, up into the heavens.
Wait. . . .

8. You are now the center of the star; as you radiate your SILVER glow you anticipate a new birth. Each breath you release extends to other stars. Your vibrations form a SILVER web which links all waiting souls together. You are anticipating the energy of life. Far away in the heavens you see a bolt of INDIGO energy coming toward you. As it approaches, your center becomes larger and larger. The INDIGO enters. Everything you are is opened and you feel new growth within.
Wait. . . .

9. Beneath you is soft grass. Your body is completely renewed. You begin to move, you feel a difference. You are small, yet

your mind is universal. All things are possible. Instead of standing, you begin to fly. You are now the Cherub of your Higher
Consciousness. You can feel your wings. Knowledge is everywhere, and you have access to all of it. As you look below, you
see your conscious self in your physical body. You long to
touch it and give it new life. It is difficult to penetrate this level.
You fly down and hear the conscious mind speaking only to
itself.
Wait. . . .

10. You touch the life energies supporting your body. It is important that you give all you can. Everything the body has
experienced—physical, mental and spiritual—is known to you.
You feel such great love and compassion as you try to make
contact. Each contact you make creates a huge burst of color.
Your very presence eliminates discord and emotional pain.
Work with your body and endeavor to make contact. Rearrange all disharmony. Each touch is deep INDIGO. Create a
new and perfect harmony around your physical body.
Wait. . . .

11. As you work with your physical body, you know the needs
and fears of the conscious level. It has separated itself from all
past knowledge. The conscious level is under great Karmic
Stress. It is in need of help. Create an INDIGO cocoon of
energy around your physical body and go to the Hall of
Records. You will have to travel back through the pain and
emotion of the conscious level. There is no need for you to feel
this pain, but realize that it is there; it is the reason for your
journey. Now travel swiftly. Move beyond the conscious restrictions to the PURPLE Hall of Records.
Wait. . . .

12. Access to this place is limited to the Higher Consciousness. It
goes beyond the Akashic Records, for it knows the beginning
and has knowledge of all things and all times. It also reveals
activity between lives. The Hall of Records stretches to the end
of the world, to the time when all souls return to the Source.
Enter the Hall and bring back what your conscious level can
understand and use for its present life situation. You will see

your companion, your MASTER, who will help and advise
you in this search.
Wait. . . .

13. Now it is time to bring your gift of knowledge back to the
conscious level. As you travel through the planes to the earth
level, you immediately feel the pull of negativity. As you make
contact, watch the body's aura reflect your arrival. See the
burst of vibrant color as you tell the conscious level what it
needs to know.
Wait. . . .

14. Now touch each chakra in turn and your energy will increase
the body's health level. As you touch the ROOT Chakra, see
vibrant RED rush to every cell. See how the body becomes
bright from the impact of your vibratory input.
Wait.

15. Touching the SACRAL Chakra, see it immediately respond.
The physical, conscious level can already feel the incoming supportive, loving energies. Bring the Sacral Chakra to perfect
balance.
Wait. . . .

16. Now concentrate fully on the UMBILICAL Chakra, which is
vulnerable to all negativity. Add strength as you project a
perfect YELLOW. See your physical body rapidly absorb what
you give.
Wait. . . .

17. Wrap yourself around the HEART Chakra and stabilize physical activity. Fill it with GREEN and see the Heart Chakra come
back to its normal balance.
Wait. . . .

18. Caress the THROAT Chakra so that the physical body may
become responsive in all these essential areas. Correct the balance of all that is heard, all that is seen and all that is spoken.
Wait. . . .

19. Now come to the INNER EYE Chakra. With your wings of
INDIGO fly to your point of inner balance. Remain there and
give peace, tranquility, balance and harmony. You are the
source of perfect balance. Fly into the VIOLET dome of wis-

dom and there find your perfect place of peace, tranquility, balance and harmony.

Wait. . . .

20. Your physical body now adjusts to its new inner balance. Every part of the body is rejuvenated. All fears are gone. You are in touch with everything you are. Peace, tranquility, balance and harmony are the gifts from the Cherub of the Higher Consciousness. Hold them, recognize them, use them and give thanks.

Say the following aloud:

I WILL RETAIN MY INNER BALANCE.
I KNOW THAT GOD EXISTS WITHIN ME.
I HAVE NO FEARS OTHER THAN WHAT I CREATE.
I AM THEE I AM. I AM THEE I AM. I AM THEE I AM.

Each day renew your Cyclotonal Level with Prayer and Affirmations.


# CYCLOTONAL PRAYER 7

## THE CHARIOT/Cyclotone 7 (VIOLET)

I must bring control into my life. My emotions have taken me in many directions. I have allowed myself to be hurt through my lack of control. I recognize the need to change my ways to find the path of divine light. I know I am capable and feel the need to be in command of my life. Today I will look directly at the things I do. I will improve my discipline. I will honestly try to discover who I am. I will break the chains of self-imposed obligations. I am turning my face to the light. Fill me with courage, give me the vision to see far ahead and realize the consequences of my weakness. I have been afraid to be me. I have pushed my sensitivity into the darkness. I have relied on my emotions and ignored many truths. I will forgive myself now and in doing so I must forgive others. The CHARIOT is my protection. I am now ready to take charge of my life. I am now responsible.

Take a few moments to feel the Presence. . . .

Now make your Affirmations to . . . THE CHARIOT.

## AFFIRMATIONS 7

1. I know my life purpose; I will make new plans in joy.
2. I must control who I am; this I will do in light.
3. I can feel my soul becoming free as I use discipline.
4. I will no longer rely on others; alone I know my way.
5. I feel new life surging inside me. I am full of light.
6. I see beyond my fears. I am protected always in light.
7. I AM THEE I AM. I AM THEE I AM. I AM THEE I AM.

## MEDITATION 21: CYCLOTONE 7/THE CHARIOT

1. Focus directly into your UMBILICAL Chakra. Breathe easily and slowly through the center of this chakra. As you release your outgoing breath, feel the power of YELLOW as it fills the entire area. Continue in this way, breathing easily and slowly. Wait. . . .

2. From this area of power see yourself in a chariot. . . . Feel the pull of the leather reins . . . the weight of your helmet . . . the ache in your physical body . . . the pain of past battles and conquest.
Wait. . . .

3. Hold your gaze directly to the front. See your life exactly as it is.
Wait. . . .

4. You are tired of battle. You must recuperate and avail yourself of healing on every possible level. The scars and wounds of life are in need of attention. Direct your chariot away from the pain and bitterness of past battles. You must take a long journey of the soul to reach the VIOLET Healing Waters. Swiftly turn your chariot toward the vast Desert of Neglect. As you ride through this barren desert, you are reminded of the many areas of your life that have been neglected. You are forced to think of all these things as you ride. Consider everything that needs attention and feel the many obligations pull at your chariot.
Wait. . . .

5. The heat and sand of the desert makes it difficult to see the oasis ahead. As the oasis comes into your vision, feel relief at leaving the desert behind you. Now you crave the refreshment of this green Spiritual Oasis. As you come closer, you forcefully bring your chariot to a halt. Ignoring others around the well, you desperately quench your thirst. Lifting your head, you see other people waiting. You walk over to the shade of a tree. Sitting and resting, you begin to notice the others who need to drink. You are curious; you shade your eyes from the sun and begin to recognize those who are drinking. You feel surprised and wonder why. Your MASTER joins you and listens to your concern. Listen well, as he reveals why these people are here.
   Wait. . . .

6. As you look again, you see some people who are unable to drink. Go and give them assistance. Hear what they have to say.
   Wait. . . .

7. Now it is time to continue your journey. Darkness is filling the sky, but you must go on. Your chariot pulls away and you travel fast as night closes in. You can see the shapes of sharp rocks; voices of your inner fears are loud in your head. Listen and understand these hidden fears. You will know that you have succeeded when each inner fear transforms through understanding into a bright star to help you on your journey.
   Wait. . . .

8. The sky above is now full of stars. Your willingness to understand your inner fears is now lighting up the heavens as you travel toward the VIOLET Healing Waters. The SUN is the center of your vehicle, the CHARIOT. The MOON is new inspiration coming into your consciousness. Holding the reins and traveling fast, you see a magnificent VIOLET SPHERE. Your mind reaches up to the VIOLET Sphere. You are eager to receive wisdom. Your chariot now lifts from the ground and you are speeding through the heavens towards the VIOLET Sphere of Wisdom. It is imperative that you reach this Sphere. Feel the Chariot rise and your mind open as you come closer. The VIOLET Sphere becomes larger and larger. A brilliant light

now pulls you and your chariot with tremendous force. You can feel the VIOLET glow of new energies. You are anxious to arrive. As you bring your chariot to a halt, you see THE ANGEL RAPHAEL with wings of PURPLE, waiting to take you to the VIOLET Dome of Wisdom. The Angel takes your hand and once again you are traveling rapidly through VIO-LET clouds. As you soar through these heavenly regions, you feel all negativity disintegrate and fall away from you.
Wait. . . .

9. The VIOLET Dome of Wisdom is on the horizon. Your feet touch the ground. You are now standing at the VIOLET Healing Waters. Submerge yourself and enjoy the healing energies on all levels of consciousness. Cleanse every atom of your being. The Angel's face becomes clearer as you bathe and remove the last fragments of negativity. Enjoy this experience. Bathe all your chakras and see them respond brilliantly to the beautiful VIOLET light.
Wait. . . .

10. You are now ready to enter the Dome of Wisdom. Your skin reflects the energies of the VIOLET Healing Waters. The Angel RAPHAEL now leads yo to the Dome. Only you can enter. Your purpose is to open your consciousness so that you can tune in to the highest vibratory frequency. Breathe in VIOLET —breathe out VIOLET. Enter the Dome of Wisdom and bring back the knowledge and understanding that you will use in your life.
Wait. . . .

11. As you leave the Dome of Wisdom, once more bathe in the VIOLET Healing Waters so that you can protect the wisdom you have received.
Wait. . . .

12. As you bathe in the purity of these Healing Waters, consider what you must do with the wisdom you have gained.
Wait. . . .

13. As you stand in the Healing Waters, a VIOLET CLOUD now comes from above and engulfs all that you are.
Wait. . . .

14. The top of your head is filling up with VIOLET rays. It feels wonderful. You realize that you are beginning to absorb the information you received. As you step out of the Healing Waters, you are in full control. You now recognize that progress is ever forward. You are totally free of Karmic Stress. You are ready to share your power and help others to renew themselves. A soul is now walking toward you. Be ready to help this soul with love, compassion and understanding. Wait. . . .

15. The Angel RAPHAEL now touches you. It is time to leave. Say goodbye and walk to the VIOLET spiral of energy. Step inside and tap its spiritual power as you breathe easily and slowly. Wait. . . .

16. Now you gradually become aware of your physical body. You have brought much power back with you. Let every part of your physical body now feel the impact of the VIOLET vibrations.
Wait. . . .

17. Complete control is now yours. Your chariot waits. It is time to rest and think how you are going to apply your new-found wisdom in your life.
Wait.

18. As you relax and feel the healing in every part of your being, give thanks.

Say the following aloud:
I GIVE THANKS FOR MY HEALING.
I AM NOW IN PERFECT CONTROL OF MY LIFE.
I WILL GIVE HEALING THROUGH WORDS AND DEEDS.
I AM THEE I AM. I AM THEE I AM. I AM THEE I AM.

Each day renew your Cyclotonal Level with Prayer and Affirmations.

CHAPTER 20

# YOUR TREE OF LIFE

Confronted as you are with the complexity of daily life, with obligations and relationships, it seems only natural to spend most of each day facing problems. Obviously these situations and people must be dealt with, but you must not allow them to govern your life. The actual source of your spiritual strength, as you now know, comes from within you. Once you begin to appreciate the vast stores of power you have at your disposal, hidden behind the masks of your everyday problems, you will be surprised at what becomes possible.

## TAKING INVENTORY

Counting your blessings against all the opposition is not easy. In fact, you seldom recognize how much energy you have available when you are busy satisfying your needs and exhausting your resources elsewhere. You need to take the time to slow down, relax and acknowledge your blessings.

When you do this, you are Taking Inventory. You will be amazed at what you have and take for granted. Your spiritual support system is often neglected and even forgotten entirely.

Recognizing who you are and analyzing your strengths is the only place to start. Present obstacles will diminish as you Take Inventory. Your new insights from this process will help eliminate Karmic Stress.

Now here is a beautiful Karmic Meditation that will enable you to truly appreciate all that you have and are.

# MEDITATION 22: ENTERING YOUR TREE OF LIFE

Like a bird, your security is in your nest. You are hidden in the leaves of your Tree of Life. Each day you fly out for food and bring back all that is needed by you and your loved ones. Your real security is in the Tree. The Tree supports the nest. Because you spend many hours building your nest, as a bird does, you invest your security in this self-made structure. The Tree of Life supports all that you build.

1. Visualize a magnificent tree. It is huge and powerful. This is your TREE OF LIFE. See where it stands, with strong branches spreading out. Walk beneath it, in the shade of its leaves, and put your arms around its trunk.
   Wait. . . .

2. Put your ear to the trunk of the Tree. Listen to the flow of sap as it comes up from the roots, through the trunk and out to every branch. See the green leaves as they constantly receive the life-giving energy. Feel the pulse of steady growth.
   Wait. . . .

3. Relax and feel yourself merge into your Tree of Life. Come into the center of the trunk. Experience the vibratory flow of life all around you.
   Wait. . . .

4. Under your feet feel the brown warmth of earth beneath the grass. The throb of nature vibrates through your feet. Your arms and fingers stretch out into every branch and leaf.
   Wait. . . .

5. Down below is the source of life. Feel the gentle pull. Your body renews itself as you sink down, down to the roots of your Tree.
   Wait. . . .

6. The ground beneath your feet is now like a velvet carpet. Stretching in every direction are vibrant SILVER energies. Up above you is the Tree. Inhale SILVER easily and slowly. Release this SILVER up, up, up into the Tree.
   Wait. . . .

7. Know that you are the source of life. Your Tree shudders in fear as it is feels the impact of cold and winter. Go up into your

Tree and bring light and comfort to every part of it. You feel the Tree tremble as the force of winter struggles against it. Wait. . . .

8. Speak to the Tree. Give it love and reassurance. It is afraid, for it is losing all its leaves. Fill the center of the Tree with power and love. Feel the Tree sway and stir in the howling wind. Once again release your energies. Let them flow into every part of the Tree.
Wait. . . .

9. A branch cracks and snaps off from the fierce impact of the wind. Immediately you sense the loss of energy. The Tree is hurt and afraid. It is dying. You are the Tree's life force. You must touch the sensitivity of this mighty Tree. You must penetrate its consciousness. Struggle and reach beyond the negative impact; fill the Tree with vibrant new energy.
Wait. . . .

10. Your Tree begins to respond. It is feeding on your love and power. Slowly it begins to ignore the outside forces. Like a baby needing its mother's milk, it now hungrily draws upon your energy. As it becomes stronger, you feel a sense of total joy. Your Tree is responding to your inner nourishment.
Wait. . . .

11. You are the spirit of your Tree. In your joy you now lift up, up, up, into every branch. As your light touches the branches, they respond eagerly with new growth. Winter has passed. YOU are spring. Now rise out of the Tree and touch all the outside branches. As your light touches them, you see new growth. Move with the sunlight in and out of the branches. Touch the trunk and feel the Tree throbbing with eternal love and gratitude.
Wait. . . .

12. You are light. Reach upward, high above your Tree. Your MASTER is waiting to show you all that you possess, all your blessings. He takes you to every blessing in your life. As you see each of these blessings, allow love and appreciation to fill your heart. Some have been neglected. Take a good, long look

at everything you have. Extend your love into areas of neglect. Rejuvenate your feelings and feel the value of all your blessings. Wait. . . .

13. Now make a sincere vow that you will not overlook the many blessings that are yours. Swear to be more attentive to the things that really matter. You are sorry for the neglect and will now treasure all that you have.
Wait. . . .

14. You are now glowing with vibrant new energies. You have changed and are happy. Down below is your Tree. It is waiting. You can feel the pull of the Tree's need as you descend toward it.
Wait. . . .

15. As you come nearer to your Tree, it reaches out into your vibratory flow; you are summer now, and the Tree has been waiting for you. Let your new radiance touch every sleeping bud. See your Tree burst into life as you dance within its branches. Feel its joy reaching out to you as you joyfully embrace your Tree of Life.
Wait. . . .

16. As your feet now touch the grass, your Tree is again high above you. Birds are busy building nests and you smile, for it is your love and power that satisfies their needs. You know the secret of life. You are the source, you are the Keeper of your Tree.
Wait. . . .

17. Completely renewed and much wiser, allow your physical body and conscious mind to absorb all that has happened. As the light now comes to your consciousness, you feel in touch with who you really are. All of your blessings are now known. Give thanks.

Say the following aloud:
I AM THE LIVING SOURCE.
I KNOW I AM WELL BLESSED.
I HAVE LOVE AND POWER.
I AM THEE I AM. I AM THEE I AM. I AM THEE I AM.

CHAPTER 21

# THE KARMIC CAUSE

We have now analyzed and determined the many sources of Karmic Stress. These stressful areas in your life can be relieved and often cured through the use of focused Karmic Meditation. The nature of your stress is colored by your karma. How is karma directly related to stress? This is an important question. Understanding the laws of karma provides the knowledge and skill to avoid unnecessary stress.

Many ancient scholars have contributed to the Hindu and Buddhist belief in reincarnation. Both Eastern and Western scholars have based their concepts and writings on similar theories. Pythagoras, Plato, Emerson, Cayce and many others have based their teachings on the principles of karma.

Basic Karmic philosophy embraces the belief that the soul survives physical death. Each soul has its own spiritual journey and is reborn again and again to perfect its earthly expression and eventually return to God. Each subsequent incarnation of the soul retains a karmic memory of the previous lifetime. Good karma enhances man's spiritual growth; he returns to earth and is reborn according to his karmic intent.

The power of the soul is capable of many things. Each life span is planned to deal specifically with only a fraction of its potential. Quite often when you think of past-life situations you tend to view the possibilities or results of a past life entirely from your present perspective. This means that you contribute a significant part of your present personality to the results of a past-life expression. A good example might be, if you were a medical doctor in your previous existence, then your reactions and thoughts about this profession might begin to project who you were then into the life of who you are now, much the same way as an actor might consider various parts he wishes to take in a play.

Each role you play in each life you live is different. Your soul designed it that way. In your present life you are trying to complete the pattern of desire selected by your soul prior to your physical birth. Imagine all the various personalities you have expressed in all your lives. If all these characters were put together, I can promise you that many would be total strangers to others.

Relationships are exactly the same. The constant need to establish a certain relationship could be caused by karmic *déjà vu*. In a previous life you could have been extremely close to this person. Another possibility is that you experienced a past relationship that was entirely different from the one you have now. The force of love impregnates itself in the soul for all time. This leaves a shadow of memory which the conscious level picks up, causing you naturally to become attracted to a person, sometimes even compelled to be with them.

Developing your ability to meditate can often solve these karmic mysteries. Your Higher Self will reveal the source of your past-life relationships. This may not happen overnight, but with the spiritual intent to learn and progress, you can discover many wonderful things about yourself. Self-discovery is the beginning of spirituality. Take a good look at your life and discard those things and situations that cause you pain. The void you may feel will become a spiritual force projecting you back to your original intent.

Your present personality does not adapt to each separate life by retaining identical traits. Karma is not a life-after-life lesson in perfecting a particular personality. The soul in its purest form is the God Essence. The adaptation of each individual life experience is the intent of the soul to shed all that prevents it from being God-like. The nature of man varies according to his talent and the circumstances of his original goal. You are not born lucky or unlucky. You come into this life as you have planned it to be. The soul is constantly in the act of seeking God. The difficulty arises when you are born into your new circumstances and limit your experience to the life you are then living. Restricting yourself to this one life-energy pattern can keep you from success.

Karmic Stress is actually a warning signal. The Higher Self observes every conscious effort you make. What you want on a conscious level is not always what your soul desires.

You encounter Karmic Stress when you allow yourself to remain in painful situations and relationships. You often tend to forget that you possess individual choice and free will. You talk about being locked into certain areas of life when in fact you are afraid to let go and leave the "security" of a negative situation. This may sound ludicrous, but it is true. Tolerance is the elasticity of the soul which allows you to move on your karmic path. Unfortunately, this gift is often misused: you hang on until you reach a devastating point that forces you to seek a new direction.

Take control now and examine your needs. Compare them with the reality of your present existence. Allow yourself time for these vital considerations. This is not a wishing space, but rather a clear area of conscious thought which will quickly show you what IS, and what COULD BE. The difference between these two realities is truly YOU, and only YOU can eliminate the pain of Karmic Stress.

# A FRIEND IN NEED

Did you really experience all that you said?
Come on now, friend, you're out of your head.
How can you tell me that you were up there?
What do you mean, you became aware?
Aware of God? Oh God forbid,
Let me tell you again there is nothing hid.
Now I believe "Two feet on the ground";
I can always see what's happening around.
My wings I will take at a later date,
I'm quite content to sit and wait.
You mentioned stress and a karmic path,
It's all so sad, it makes me laugh.
Your fears have gone, just tell me where.
You can't change things, life's just not fair.
Let me say right here and now,
If you really can, please show me how.

—Eileen Connolly

# RECORDING MEDITATIONS

This section is intended for both teachers and students. It is important to allow sufficient time for physical and mental relaxation. To reach the required levels you must be in a state of relaxation. Teachers may consider using soft music in the background to facilitate these requirements. Make sure that all clothing is loose and anything that may cause discomfort is removed prior to the relaxation period.

You will see after each statement the word "WAIT." The sensitive teacher will understand what the students are trying to achieve at that particular moment and allow adequate time for them to experience fully each phase of the meditation. The student who undertakes to work alone should also allow sufficient time between each step. When recording the instructions, keep this in mind.

All the meditations in this book are available on tape. They can be used both in classwork and at home. For further information regarding tapes and advanced studies, contact the University at the address below.

Connolly University of Parapsychology
Box 76, Richmond Road
Lanexa, VA 23089

# EILEEN CONNOLLY'S MYSTICAL FOCHAADAMS

The MYSTICAL FOCHAADAMS are a new and exciting form of divination which can reveal esoteric wisdom and guidance through the interpretations of the symbols portrayed. Eileen Connolly, author, lecturer and teacher, has spent years researching and developing this unique system. In 1974 she named them with a mystical word derived from two languages, Hebrew and Tibetan:

| | | |
|---|---|---|
| FO | Fohat | Essence of cosmic electricity |
| CHAA | Chabad | Wisdom, reason and intuition |
| DAMS | Yidams | Phenomenal projections of a person's inherent energy |

Like many other forms of divination—Tarot, Numerology, Astrology, etc.—the Mystical Fochaadams are not to be considered as a means of mere fortune-telling, but rather as a modern tool to help you discover, analyze and make meaningful decisions based on your higher level of consciousness. Throwing the Mystical Fochaadams and being prepared to recognize future trends as the results of present activities will lead you into areas of interpretation that will greatly enhance your esoteric skill, sensitivity and intuition.

Ancient symbols were designed to lead the higher consciousness into esoteric areas without the restrictions of form and reason. They were intended to trigger the student's higher vibrations, thus opening his awareness to areas of philosophy hitherto unknown to him. Various images and shapes formed the languages of the ancients. The discovery of how certain symbols, like words, have been used by many different cultures was the key to mastering the whole system.

Words can often obliterate the vast knowledge contained in symbology. Working with symbols eliminates the need for words as such, allowing emotion in its purest form to reach and stimulate the higher senses directly.

The Mystical Fochaadams allow access into the world of esoteric wisdom and can give you the ability to understand and make use of this wisdom, based on your own personal level of sensitivity. Master the Mystical Fochaadams and you will always have a friend. Like the Tarot, they can be used both for yourself or with clients.

Your Mystical Fochaadams consist of a beautiful esoteric throw cloth and a collection of unique updated symbols on a group of throwing pieces. They are simple to use and can reveal the past, present and future with amazing accuracy.

The Mystical Fochaadams enchance and complement other divination systems: they can confirm and clarify many areas of interest opened by the Tarot, answering questions regarding relationships, business, financial matters, etc. You will find them an invaluable addition to your esoteric tools and discover an oracle of hitherto unsuspected dimensions.

Dr. Connolly also conducts International Certification Courses in the following subjects: Gnothology, Tarot, and esoteric philosophy.

* Lectures
* Workshops
* Intensive Study
* Seminars
* Tapes

For information on wholesale and retail sales and courses, write to:

Eileen Connolly Associates, Inc.
Box 19, Richmond Road
Lanexa, VA 23089